Jesus Cropped from the Picture

Why Christians Get Bored
And How to Restore Them to Vibrant Faith

Don Allsman

The Urban Ministry Institute is a ministry of World Impact, Inc.

All Scripture quotations, unless otherwise noted, are from The Holy Bible, English Standard Version, copyright © 2001 by Crossway Bible, a division of Good News Publishers. Used by permission. All Rights Reserved.

Photos used by permission courtesy of *Yankton Press and Dakotan*, P.O. Box 56, Yankton, South Dakota 57078.

Acknowledgments

To Cathy

Your vibrant faith in Christ and your steadfast love toward others has inspired me these 25 years we have shared together.

The delightful aspect of researching this book is that it was done in conversation with friends. The *Granville Group* (Rick Durrance, Brian Morrison, Bob Drummond, and Dave Evans), the *Epic* class, and the *How We Do Church* group (Brad Brown, Dave Rutledge, Glenn Gilmore, and Tyler McCauley) gave shape to the ideas that are articulated in this book. Special thanks goes to Jeanie Hamilton, who labored so much to help me edit this book.

- Don Allsman
March 2010

About the Author

Don Allsman is Vice President of World Impact and Satellite Director of The Urban Ministry Institute, World Impact's urban leadership development center. Don earned a Bachelor of Science in Industrial Engineering from *California State University, Fresno* and a Master of Business Administration from *The Wichita State University*. Don and his wife Cathy have been missionaries with World Impact since 1991 and have two sons, Ryan and Mark. Don is also the author of **The Heroic Venture: A Parable of Project Leadership**, available at www.tumi.org.

Contents

Part Three: Back to the Future

Appendices

Introduction

I love churches!

My love for all kinds of churches comes not just from my affection for Jesus, but also because I am an executive with World Impact, a missions organization whose aim is to plant churches cross-culturally among America's urban poor. World Impact missionaries live incarnationally in the urban areas where we plant churches and minister to the whole person through schools, camps, medical clinics, and the distribution of food and clothing.

I am also the Satellite Director for The Urban Ministry Institute (TUMI), World Impact's theological and leadership development ministry for those lacking access to traditional seminary education due to cost, admission requirements, proximity, or cultural relevance. At TUMI, we train urban pastors and elders who are committed to biblical, historic, orthodox faith from a variety of faith traditions.

So it is not surprising that I love churches who are faithful to the Lord Jesus: traditional, emerging, charismatic, Reformed, evangelical, or liturgical. The list could go on. But across all lines of Christian heritage, there is a growing and fearful consensus that Christian faith is *declining in America*. At the same time, all accounts suggest an explosion of vibrancy in other parts of the world, such as Latin America, Asia, and Africa.

Over the past decades, I have observed these divergent trends from two perspectives. First, I am training pastors and missionaries to plant healthy churches in a variety of cultural environments in urban America. Second, I am a member of a suburban evangelical church. This "double life" has allowed me to experience a world of dynamic and invigorating Christian living in my urban context, while observing a precipitating sense of boredom, discouragement, and shallowness in my suburban church setting.

In recent years I have talked with other church leaders and researched as much as I could to discover the underlying causes of these two opposing experiences. I have been eager to identify why one world is characterized by *courage and spiritual vitality*, while the other is descending into *boredom and lethargy*.

My concern was this: if there is something inherently unhealthy in America's suburban (and rural) churches, the mentors they send to The Urban Ministry Institute might be exporting that same spiritual identity into the training we are offering urban church leaders. I wondered if the message they were bringing with them was defective in some way. As Rick Wood said, "This would be like Bill Gates sending out the latest Microsoft operating system which after installed for a year deletes all the files on the computer.... If the Gospel we proclaim will self-destruct once installed on the hard drives of people's hearts, then much of our work among the unreached peoples could be in danger of collapse as it has in much of Europe."[1]

This concern grew into a passion that motivated me to uncover the sources of this "two-world" phenomenon. *Jesus Cropped from the Picture is my attempt to help inner-city pastors avoid the boredom and lethargy of*

America's suburban churches, while proposing ways to enhance their spiritual vibrancy.

Part One: This Provincial Life describes my analysis of the decline of the American church over the past few decades, as it slowly reduced from *participation in Christ's Kingdom Story*, to a system oriented to the *personal needs of the Self*. This system is too narrow and constraining (provincial) to maintain enthusiasm, producing Christians suffering from boredom, burnout, or despondency.

Part Two: Do You Know Where You're Going To? represents my perspective of how this *self-oriented* system was formed by the blending of American marketing principles and the good intentions of believers seeking to advance the cause of Christ. This system took shape in three contemporary methods, each seeking to re-invigorate the church: *Traditional*, *Pragmatic*, and *Emerging*.

Part Three: Back to the Future explains how *methods* to build the church ultimately crop Jesus from the big picture of Scripture. The best way to restore Christians to vibrant faith is to recapture the Church's *identity* as "People of the Story" by re-connecting to our *sacred roots*, articulated in the Great Tradition.

I am indebted to Rev. Dr. Don Davis, Director of The Urban Ministry Institute, and fellow World Impact Vice President. His vision and tutelage framed my understanding, so this book is simply my testimony of his teaching as it has been borne out in my experience over several years.

I am also grateful for the many hours of discussion with Dr. Rick Durrance, Senior Pastor at Emmanuel Church. Without his insight I would not have been able to articulate my observations.

My personal angst took me on a journey where I had to suspend judgment to gain insight about my assumptions. I was surprised by the depth of those presuppositions. Therefore, I encourage readers to suspend their judgment until the conclusion of the book.

I know my explanations come from my own experience and that many readers may find various aspects at odds with their own. Because I am trying to describe a wide range of historical periods and Christian traditions, space limitations force me to make broad generalizations at the risk of drawing offensive caricatures. My summaries of Church history, Christian movements, and faith traditions are presented with humility, for the purpose of creating clearly-understood categories that open the way for Christ to be exalted and bored Christians restored to vibrant faith.

Despite my oversimplifications, my prayer is that you will be *stunned* by the ingenious plan of the Father, *refreshed* by a broader appreciation of the Lord Jesus Christ, and *confident* that your church can experience new adventure under the guidance of the Holy Spirit.

Part One: This Provincial Life

"There must be more than this provincial life!"

- Belle, _Beauty and the Beast_

....

The American church is in decline because Christianity has been reduced from "participation in God's Story" to a system oriented to the personal needs of individuals. This system is too narrow and constraining (provincial) to maintain enthusiasm, producing Christians who are bored, burned-out, or despondent.

Chapter 1: Why Is That Old Man Crying?

IN JUNE 2005 I scheduled a visit to Wichita with my long-time friend Brian, an associate pastor from the Midwest. What started off as a pleasant weekend turned into an historic event in my life.

Since 1991, when I was called to missionary service with World Impact, I have lived in two worlds. For years, my wife Cathy and I had been volunteers with World Impact when suddenly, with only a few days' notice, I was asked to become their Vice President of Administration. With our first child (Ryan) on the way, we were in no position to abruptly move into the inner-city community where the other World Impact-Los Angeles missionaries lived. So we began our work in the city while living 12 miles away as members of an evangelical church in Burbank.

Over the years, the differences between my two worlds grew. Subconsciously, I sensed the gap widening. My local church experience was becoming more shallow, more thin, less stimulating, while my life in the inner city was challenging, exciting, and invigorating (sometimes more challenging than I wanted).

Some would say it was a difference between missionaries (who are serious and called) versus a local church (comprised of a mixture of both committed and passive believers). But I knew it was more than that. I knew too many faithful believers at my local church to draw such a conclusion. They loved Christ, had a high view of his Word, and were sincerely concerned about others. I knew there was something deeper taking place.

I also starting hearing rumblings from other church leaders from a variety of traditions and denominations. For example, a Presbyterian manual reported their observations about the church in America: "Some 85% will self-identify as Christians. Yet less than 40% of Americans attend church with any regularity. They believe—they just don't go. They see no point. They have tried church … And they have decided to stay home with the paper and a cup of coffee.... Over 70 million persons in America believe in God and would join a church if they could find one they liked!"[2]

George Barna wrote, "Driven out of their longtime church by boredom and the inability to serve in ways that made use of their considerable skills and knowledge, they spent some time exploring other churches. After months of honest effort, neither found a ministry that was sufficiently stimulating and having an impact on the surrounding community."[3]

Reggie McNeal added, "A growing number of people are leaving the institutional church for a new reason. They are not leaving because they lost their faith. They are leaving to preserve their faith."[4]

At the same time, I began to hear about the explosion of the Church in other parts of the world, such as Latin America, Asia, and Africa. For example, David Wells said:

Here in the West, Christianity is stagnant, but in Africa, Latin America, and parts of Asia, it is burgeoning, at least statistically. The statistical center of gravity of the Christian Church worldwide has moved out of Europe and is now found in northern Africa. The face of Christianity is changing as a result. It is no longer predominantly northern, European, and Anglo-Saxon. Its face is that of the underdeveloped world. It is predominantly from the Southern hemisphere, young, quite uneducated, poor, and very traditional. The question Westerners need to ponder is why, despite our best efforts at cultural accommodation in America, God seems to be taking his work elsewhere."[5]

Bob Roberts summed it up this way: "Regardless of the religious right and despite the emergence of mega-churches, postmodern churches, and house churches, nothing has stemmed the tide of Christianity's slow decline in the West. We continue to decline while the Church is simultaneously exploding in the East as the world has never known."[6]

As I watched this phenomenon out of the corner of my eye, I was increasingly puzzled, but not sufficiently motivated to investigate the causes. I was too busy carrying out my missionary call in the inner city to give it much thought. Then I met Brian in Wichita.

He was going through a challenging season in his life, feeling that church life was becoming untenable. He still loved Christ, but the church was sapping his strength. As a pastor, the task of infusing life into his church was increasingly difficult. We spent the weekend trying to articulate what we both were experiencing in our local church settings.

Like many people, Brian was tired of the institutions and routines that seemed to block a refreshing life in Christ. He was worn out from endless programs and practices that did little to draw people close to Christ.

Despite my best effort to encourage Brian, I was not much help. I was discouraged myself, and frustrated by my inability to identify the sources of our consternation. I said goodbye to him at the airport, departing without resolution.

On the flight back to Los Angeles, I determined to get to the bottom of this issue. Experiencing Brian's dismay changed my perspective. This was no longer theoretical. *It was personal.*

So I started a headlong pursuit of prayer, study, and dialogue. I tried to hear from everyone I could. I pleaded with God to help me understand. During the last half of 2005, my discouragement deepened as I noticed friends growing increasingly bored and withdrawn. I was sinking. I hit bottom in December 2005 at a Disney stage production of *Beauty and the Beast.*[7]

Sitting with my wife and two sons, I was deep in thought. I asked myself, "What is it about the American church that produces such shallowness, superficiality, and church-hopping? What are the cultural and historical roots of this phenomenon?" Then suddenly, I became aware of the singer portraying Belle, as she verbalized the feelings that were welling up in me: her disappointment in the quiet monotony of her village, her painful longing for her neighbors to experience adventure outside their mundane existence, and her cry to escape her provincial life.

As I listened to her words about "This Provincial Life," I sheepishly wiped the tears from my eyes, wondering if the little girl next to me was whispering to her mother, "Mommy, why is that old man crying?" At that moment, I asked the Lord to help me articulate a way out of the provincial life I was seeing in the American church.

It was not long before God answered that prayer, and it all started coming together. I began to see two foundational patterns that gave shape to "this provincial life."

Chapter 2: Cropping the Picture

THE STORY OF God's interaction with his creation is revealed in the Bible. There is a storyline in the Scriptures that moves from beginning to end (Genesis to Revelation). The plot of this unfolding drama is now being lived out in the history of the Church until Jesus returns (see Appendix 1). As C.S. Lewis said, "Christianity is the story of how a rightful king has landed, you might say in disguise, and is calling us all to take part in a great campaign of sabotage."[8]

The image in Figure 1, depicted by two competing basketball players, symbolizes this historic understanding of Christian faith. The primary subject of the scene is the basketball player holding a ball, driving past his opponent.

Figure 1: The Full Picture

This picture illustrates Christian faith in that the player holding the ball represents Christ and his Kingdom purpose: "The reason the Son of God appeared was to destroy the work of the devil" (1 John 3.8). The defensive player represents the devil, the key figure of the opposing "kingdom of this world." The basketball in the hands of the player represents the Church, of whom Jesus is head.

In the picture, the offensive player is the *primary subject*, the defensive player is the *secondary subject*, and the ball is the *object*. In the biblical narrative of the Kingdom, <u>Jesus</u> is the *primary* **SUBJECT,** the devil is the *secondary subject*, and the <u>Church</u> is the **OBJECT**.

Slowly over time, the American church changed its perspective of Christ's Kingdom Story by "cropping" the picture to look like Figure 2.

Figure 2: The Partially Cropped Picture

The photo in Figure 2 is the same photo as Figure 1, but two dynamics were at work to create this new perspective. First, a <u>choice</u> was made to focus on *one part* of the photo (the basketball), to the exclusion of other parts of the photo. Second, a <u>process</u> (cropping) was employed to exclude the two players from the photo so that only the hands of the player remained (see Figure 3).

Figure 3: Fully Cropped Picture

The original, complete picture (see Figure 1) was slowly eliminated until only the cropped photo remained (see Figure 3). This process did not happen all at once, but in slow increments, over many centuries. Jesus remained a player in the photo, but he became the "supplier of my needs," the *hands holding the basketball*. He became the **OBJECT** and was no longer the **SUBJECT**. Michael Horton said, "To increasing millions of Americans, God ... exists for the pleasure of humankind. He resides in the heavenly realm solely for our utility and benefit."[9]

The other basketball player, representing the devil and his kingdom, was also cropped from the picture. To various degrees, Satan's "kingdom of this world" became largely irrelevant.

What is left after the cropping process is a *Self* that is prominent (the basketball), a God who exists to care for the *Self* (the hands holding the ball), and no larger context to see where *any of this Story is going*. There is no adversary. There is no point. It is static. As he holds the ball, it is unclear if the basketball player is in action or standing still.

This "cropping" process was conducted by the well-intentioned efforts of sincere Christians who wanted to make Christ known and advance his purposes in the world. But their work had unforeseen implications.

First, over many centuries, the **SUBJECT** changed from Christ as *Victorious Lord* to Christ as *Savior of the Church*. Then, gradually, the **SUBJECT** changed from Christ the "Savior of the Church" to Christ "my personal savior." Jesus was essentially demoted from Victorious

Jesus Cropped from the Picture

Lord, to Savior of the Church, to my personal savior. This made the *Self* the new SUBJECT (Individualism).

Second, analytical approaches were employed to simplify the gospel message for broader acceptance and mass communication (Rationalism). These two historic and cultural forces (Rationalism and Individualism) worked together to *crop Jesus from the picture* of his own Story.

The "cropping" process is deeper than human selfishness. People in *all* cultures have been selfish. Selfishness is not new. However, a *culture oriented around the Self* is a recent American innovation. Americans are taught to be self-oriented, and it is unlikely the culture will change. But within American self-oriented culture, Christians can choose to act either *selfishly* or *unselfishly*. People can be unselfish, even while they live in a self-oriented culture.

Therefore, the problem is not asking people to be less selfish. It is not enough to say, "It's not about me, it's all about him" (not being selfish). There is something far deeper than unselfishness. **The problem is that the Story is too small.** The solution is to restore the Story to its full picture so Christians can find a new identity, where Jesus is the SUBJECT again.

Chapter 3: The First Cropping Tool: Individualism

IN A DESIRE to bring people to Christ, innovative approaches have been employed to reduce the message so it could be easily understood and communicated. Using effective methods of American advertising, Christians formulated a host of ways to share the gospel, resulting in countless numbers of people coming to Christ. But these methods had unintended consequences.

The Hearer As the Main Character

The process of simplifying the *Story of the Kingdom* omitted some of the key elements of the Story. Getting the message into a tight presentation retained Jesus as Savior, but placed the potential convert at the *center* of discussion. Evangelism was conducted to get the person to "accept Christ" in a way that caused hearers to infer that they were the central character in the discussion. Instead of inviting people to "join Christ's Kingdom," language was used that put the *hearer at the center.*

From their first introduction to Christ, new Christians have been trained to understand the gospel of the Kingdom in a self-oriented way. The contrast between "accept Jesus into your life," and "join in what Christ is doing," is profound.

For example, the image in Figure 4 shows how there are two ways of perceiving something. If the background is viewed to be white, the black candlestick seems obvious. But if the observer sees a black background, it becomes apparent that two faces are looking at each other.

Figure 4: Black or White Background

Also, the picture in Figure 5 can appear to be either a young woman looking away, or an old woman in profile.

Figure 5: Two Women

These two simple examples illustrate how a message can be understood in radically different ways. Similarly, Americans changed the perspective from *Christ* being central to *Self* being central.

One striking illustration is the potential misunderstanding of <u>Campus Crusade's</u> *Four Spiritual Laws,*[10] a presentation used by God to bring millions to faith in Christ in recent decades (see Figure 6). The individual (the circle) can be misconceived as the **SUBJECT** of the image because it is the largest part of the graphic (the main subject of

Spiritual Person (Christ-Directed Life)
Jesus is in the life and on the throne. Self is yielding to Jesus. The person sees Jesus' influence and direction in their life.

Figure 6: Individual or Christ?

conversation). Christ, while seated on the throne of the individual, can be inferred as the **OBJECT**, because the cross is smaller than the circle.

People viewing this presentation could erroneously view themselves as the **SUBJECT**, and see Christ as the **OBJECT**. "Me and my personal relationship with Christ" becomes the message. Christ and his Kingdom is made secondary to "my individual decision-making about Christ's role in my life." The invitation to *join his Kingdom* can easily be lost on a person who is already looking at life through a self-oriented lens.

Despite the warning of Campus Crusade that sin is what causes people to put *Self* on the throne, the observer can infer that *Self is the Sovereign,* the one in a position to employ Jesus or not.

This notion has been reinforced through thousands of books, sermons, Bible studies, and radio broadcasts. A constant diet of *me at the center, with Christ there to help me* has slowly cropped the photo until people see themselves as the **SUBJECT** (the basketball), and Christ as the **OBJECT** (the hands holding the basketball).

Michael Horton said: "The focus still seems to be on us and our activity rather than on God and his work in Jesus Christ. Across the board from conservative to liberal, Roman Catholic to Anabaptist, New Age to Southern Baptist, the 'search for the sacred' in America is largely oriented to what happens inside of us, in our personal experience rather than in what God has done for us in history."[11]

Slowly, the Christian life became less about Christ's global purposes and more about his specific task to save the Church from punishment. Eventually it was not even about his Church (with "me" as a crucial part of the Church). Instead, the Church is viewed as a collection of individual Christians, each with their own *personal relationships with Christ,* gathering together to get their individual needs met.

Christian Sans Church

For some, even church became optional and was completely cropped from the picture. Recently, a group of Christians passed out gospel tracts at the middle school where my son (Mark) attends. The final pages of the tract highlighted the need to *believe in Jesus, pray to Jesus, read the Bible, and spread the word.* The Church was never mentioned. Clearly, Christ is "in," but the Church is "out."

The implication is, "If you can get your needs met without church, why bother? If books, television, radio, or podcasts can meet personal your spiritual needs, why go to a local church?" George Barna provides a shocking example of how far the *cropping process* has degenerated when he said:

> Whether you become a Revolutionary immersed in, minimally involved in, or completely disassociated from a local church is irrelevant to me (and, within boundaries, to God). What matters is not whom you associate with (i.e. a local church), but who you are.... The Bible neither describes nor promotes the local church as we know it today.... It does, however, offer direction regarding the importance and integration of fundamental spiritual disciplines into one's life.... Ultimately, we

expect to see believers choosing from a proliferation of options, weaving together a set of favored alternatives into a unique tapestry that constitutes the personal 'church' of the individual.... It seems that God doesn't really care how we honor and serve him, as long as he is number one in our lives and our practices are consistent with his parameters. If a local church facilitates that kind of life, then it is good. And if a person is able to live a godly life outside of a congregation-based faith, then that, too, is good.[12]

For many like Barna, being a "Christian without the Church" is no longer dubious, but encouraged. The problem is that the *Story of Christ and his Kingdom* makes no sense outside of a local church. Gordon Fee said:

> More than anything, the church is a group of former sinners joined together in Christ, filled with the Holy Spirit, on a mission … In fact, the New Testament knows nothing of individualistic salvation; much of what God calls us to do cannot be done apart from community. People are always saved into community. Helping each other, working together in a common cause, praying together, teaching one another, and supporting each other in our weaknesses and trials all mean that we become deeply involved with each other's lives. Church is not a place we attend. Church is a community we belong to.[13]

<u>The Role of the Individual</u>

The *cropped picture* that makes *Self* the **SUBJECT** is a recent American invention, having no biblical precedence. Still, some try to express faith this way: "My true self is known by what is unique about <u>me</u>. The community exists for me to discover myself. Christ is 'my' savior, and salvation provides me a one-on-one personal relationship with God, who speaks to me individually. I can decide to make him Lord of my life or not."

In contrast, a biblical understanding sounds more like this: "My true self is known by the groups I associate with, so I find value in my connections with those groups, not in my unique personal qualities. I am responsible to the community, it is not there just to meet my needs. I am part of the body of Christ, where Jesus is head, so salvation makes me a member of a community, where I am adopted into a family. Most often, God speaks to me through the community, not to me personally. Through baptism, I publically declare my allegiance to the Kingdom of God as a lasting sign of commitment to Christ and his family."[14]

<u>Unspoken Misery</u>
Despite the decline in attendance, many believers *do* stay committed to the local church. However, if they would admit it, they often do so out of a *sense of duty*.

Oriented around the belief that *me and my personal relationship* is what Christian faith is about, believers approach worship, study, and fellowship to receive. So the key question they are taught is, "How does this apply to me?"

This orientation around *Self* produces a variety of internal responses: "Church is boring to me sometimes. The church does not meet my needs. Maybe I should find a different church. Sometimes I do not get much from my Bible reading. I do not feel fed by this pastor. The programs do not meet my needs. The people are not helping me grow spiritually."

People who make such statements show that Jesus may have been *cropped from their picture*. Their problems are not necessarily the fault of the church, the pastor, or the programs, but with their *Self-orientation*. The individual has become the **SUBJECT**, and Jesus has become the **OBJECT**. Bob Roberts said, "The individualistic, narcissistic, consumer mind-set that has gripped the church today is killing us."[15]

There is a humorous illustration of this consumer mind-set at youtube.com called, Drive-Through Church.[16] It would be hilarious if it were not so painfully *accurate*. In a series of vignettes, drivers pull up to what looks like a fast-food drive-through. However, each car is actually pulling up to order what they want from church. The person on the speaker asks, "How can we feed you today?"

One person asks for a good parking space in the shade; another for a 25-minute inspiring sermon, but not too challenging; a third person asks for three clapping songs, but no handshaking with new people. Another man drives up and asks who the preacher is that day. When told, "Pastor Wilkes," he begins to drive away, saying, "I'm not so crazy about him." When the voice recants and mentions a different preacher, the man backs up his car and says, "That's more like it."

In contrast to the "Drive-Through Church" that produces bored Christians, the un-cropped picture of *Christ and his Story* (see Figure 1) is producing vibrancy among the poor where there is not a cultural orientation around the *Self*. A Christ-centered, Kingdom-oriented perspective says, "Church services are not for me, they are to honor Christ. The Church exists to fulfill Christ's purposes, and the task of the individual is to help him carry out those purposes." When reading the Bible and hearing sermons, the key question is not, "*How does this apply to me?*" but rather, "*Why is this important to God?*"

Christians oriented around the Kingdom are joyfully committed to their local church because they see themselves in a larger context, trusting God to lead and feed them through their pastors and teachers, forgiving others when offended, and giving themselves in worship rather than focusing on *Self*. An orientation to the Kingdom is vital to *de-cropping the picture*.

But what exactly is "the Kingdom of God?"

Chapter 4: The Kingdom of God

IN THE PREVIOUS chapter, Individualism was described as the change in orientation:

- from "Jesus and his Kingdom" to "me and my personal relationship"
- from "the Kingdoms in conflict" to "Jesus being there for me"

Individualism was the <u>decision</u> to crop *Jesus and his Kingdom* from the picture, making Jesus the **OBJECT** (the hands holding the basketball).

In this fully cropped picture, the adversary is absent. But the Kingdom of God makes sense only when there is an adversarial kingdom. DeYoung and Hurty claimed, "All the world is a stage, it has been said. In no sense is this more true than in the great drama being played out which we might call the 'Conflict of the Ages.' The plot in Scripture and history reveals a cosmic war between two kingdoms in which we are all playing a part according to God's plan. It is against this backdrop of God's Kingdom purpose in history that biblical writers have both written and interpreted Scripture."[17] In fact, the entire biblical account is a *Story of conflict between good and evil.*[18]

The Kingdom of God is the single, continuous action of God to restore all that was destroyed by the Fall. At the incarnation of Jesus, the King landed in enemy territory. Through his temptation and miracles, Jesus of Nazareth delivered a series of defeats to the devil. By his blood, Christ rescued a people to be his own, and his resurrection dealt a crippling blow to the powers of evil. The Kingdom is now here (Matt. 12:28).

However, there are still many knees that have not bowed, nor tongues confessed, to the Kingship of Jesus (Phil. 2.10-11). Until that happens, the Kingdom is not fully consummated. There is still work to be done before Jesus returns to obliterate the *kingdom of this world*. The Kingdom is also "not-yet."

Jesus' Favorite Topic

Most scholars agree that the Kingdom of God was Jesus' favorite topic. He refers to the Kingdom 130 times in the gospels. There are many excellent ways to explore, define and discuss the Kingdom of God,[19] and no one summary needs to be definitive. However the following definition of the Kingdom is helpful to me:

> **The Kingdom of God is the progressive expansion of God's life-giving rule over creation, until all things are under his perfect ruling authority.**

This definition has three dimensions that make up the overall story of the Bible:

1. The Throne. Jesus re-takes his rightful place on the throne as King over all. *"The kingdom of the world has become the kingdom of our Lord and of his Christ, and he shall reign for ever and ever (Rev. 11.15)."*

2. The Conquest. Jesus destroys his enemy, the devil, and casts him to eternal punishment, along with all who had followed the devil.

"Then comes the end, when he delivers the kingdom to God the Father after destroying every rule and authority and power. For he must reign until he has put all his enemies under his feet (1 Cor. 15.24-25)."

3.   The Rescue. Jesus rescues a people to be his own bride. *"He has delivered us from the domain of darkness and transferred us to the kingdom of his beloved Son (Col. 1.13)."*

In their well-meaning efforts to reduce the Story to an easy-to-communicate message, many traditions have minimized the first two aspects (Throne and Conquest), and focused almost exclusively on the third (Rescue), limiting a full understanding of Scripture. In some cases the Throne and Conquest are downplayed on purpose, because people are uncomfortable with those aspects of the Story. In either case, the Rescue (without the Throne and Conquest) has now become the heart of the Christian message in America.

With the devil cropped out of the picture, the individual (the basketball) takes on greater importance than is intended, and the picture makes little sense. The picture is too small. Rather than focusing on the broad aspects of the Story (a King who regains his throne against an evil adversary), the emphasis has been on a Rescuer *who saves the individual.*

While it is true that a Rescue is being made, there is too much emphasis on the individual, which blurs the Story. God's plan "includes not only the reconciliation of people to God, but the reconciliation of 'all things in heaven and on earth.' The redemption of persons is at the center of God's plan, but it is not the *circumference* of that plan."[20]

Two Views of the Rescue

Another way people have tried to create an easier-to-communicate message is by narrowing the many aspects of Jesus' victory over the powers of evil (the atonement) to one representative act, namely his work at the cross *for personal salvation.*

Without question, Jesus' substitutionary work on the cross is the crowning achievement of his atonement, and should not be diminished in any way (Col. 1.20). However, Jesus not only gave his life on the cross, but also defeated the devil through his incarnation, victory in the wilderness temptation, sinless life, clarification of Old Testament teachings, miracles of exorcism, delegation of authority to the disciples, resurrection, and ascension. He continues to conquer the enemy through his mediation as head of the Church, and will complete the conquest at his Second Coming[21] when he will put "all things under his feet" (Eph. 1.22).

Jesus did far more to "destroy the works of the devil" (1 John 3.8) than securing personal salvation at the cross, glorious as it is! The full portfolio of Jesus' work is far more than just *my rescue at the cross.* Robert Webber noted, "The sacrifice of himself for the reconciliation of the world was already taking place in the womb of the Virgin Mary."[22]

For the first 1000 years of the Church, this "multi-dimensional" appreciation of Jesus' many victories over the devil was recognized by the title "Christus Victor"[23] (Christ the Victor). At the Reformation, Luther attempted to revive the Christus Victor notion by emphasizing that Jesus' work was not limited to the cross, but continues during the Church age, until he returns.[24]

But in recent times, the Christus Victor view virtually vanished from the American church, where Jesus' work is often reduced almost exclusively to his death and resurrection, as a means toward personal salvation. Ignoring his other accomplishments, and reducing the cross to **personal salvation**, has *cropped Jesus out of the picture.*

One-Dimensional Implications

Reducing the work of Jesus to *the cross (for personal salvation)* had far-reaching implications for people in a self-oriented environment. It suggested a static, provincial view of life. For example, it was not farfetched to conclude that "since Jesus did the work on the cross, now all the work is done. I can accept Christ, live a moral life, and wait until heaven, living an ethical life out of a *thankful response* to his Rescue (personal salvation). As long as I avoid sin, learn facts about the Bible, and share the story of the Rescue with others, my duty is fulfilled."

Taking this error further, some have concluded, "Since Jesus suffered and died in my place, I do not have to suffer. In fact, as long as I do my job (avoid sin, accumulate good doctrine, share the gospel, and pray), God will make my life good."

When these assumptions take root, believers are susceptible to easy-believism, license, or laziness. When pastors see such lack of discipline, they feel pressure to use rules and guilt to motivate people.

On the other hand, since no one can ever do enough to show a truly *thankful response* for their <u>Rescue</u>, people are easy prey to legalism and false guilt. These faulty assumptions put too much pressure on people, creating discouragement. They become lazy or overworked, neither of which is what God intended for his Church.

Multi-Dimensional Implications

By focusing on the broad range of Jesus' work before, during, and after the cross, it is clear that Jesus continues to destroy the works of the devil today, through the Church, the agent of his Kingdom (see Appendix 2).

However, the Church is not the Kingdom, nor the King. Jesus alone "has bound, dethroned, and will ultimately destroy all the powers of evil and will restore the created order."[25] God is actively working to restore his Kingdom on the earth, and he does this with or without the intentional participation of his people. But the Church is Jesus' chosen agent to carry on his work in the world, through the power of the Holy Spirit. The Church is the **OBJECT** of God's enterprise.

Therefore, anyone who repents and believes is now qualified to join the Church in destroying the work of the devil until Jesus returns. Once saved, a person's work is not over; *it has just begun* (see Appendix 3). Sin is to be avoided, not just out of a *thankful response* for their <u>Rescue</u>, but because sin is aiding and abetting the enemy's kingdom. Anyone who prays, "Your Kingdom come, your will be done, on earth as it is in heaven," is asking God to expand his rule, through the Church, in this present age. This prayer is an invitation to join in the fray.

Christians are <u>Rescued</u> because there is a *task to be performed*. The Church participates in God's mission to actualize his Kingdom on earth. God sanctifies believers, conforming them to the image of his Son, making them increasingly effective in the task of destroying the devil's work (Rom. 8.28-29).

But the Church needs weapons to do God's work. The Holy Spirit gifts believers to make the Church more potent against the kingdom of this world. "The Spirit has come to empower us to continue the invasion of the kingdom."[26]

All elements of church life are rooted in the continual effort to reverse the devil's work to *steal, kill, and destroy* (Jn. 10.10). Theology, worship, discipleship, and outreach should be integrated into the Church's overall purpose to be the agent of Christ's victorious Kingdom. In this light, social action <u>and</u> personal evangelism are important Kingdom activities. **The gospel should be both demonstrated and declared.**

From this perspective, suffering can also be understood differently. Like Paul, believers can know the "joy of the fellowship of his suffering" (Phil. 3.10), by being baptized into his death, joining in the vigorous conflict Jesus began. This view leaves no time for laziness or easy-believism, because there is cosmic work to be done every day. Because Jesus released his people from a religious standard (Gal. 5.1), there is freedom in Christ to forgive others, exercise spiritual gifts, pursue relationships, and plot innovative ways to do good in the world, without overworking or burning out.

Dr. Don Davis likes to say that the Story of the Kingdom should produce a breath-taking wonder in his people, which should lead to worship of this amazing God. Then, out of that worship, believers should be moved to sacrificial work. **Wonder leads to worship, and worship leads to work.**

But because Christ himself will achieve victory over the devil at his Second Coming, believers have no reason to put inordinate pressure on themselves to do everything. The Christian life can become a dynamic, vibrant life, full of adventure, where his people contribute to his Kingdom purposes with freedom and joy. The Kingdom of God frees Christians from "this provincial life."

A Single Coherent Center

There has been debate over the existence of a single coherent center, where all the seemingly unrelated *questions and issues of life* make sense under one idea (see Figure 7).

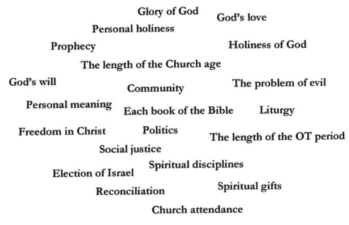

Figure 7: Seeking Coherence

In the absence of an overriding coherent center, Christians in a self-oriented environment are likely to craft their own version of coherence by making "my personal relationship" the circle that encompasses the *questions and issues of life*. The problem is "my personal relationship" is too small to make sense of all the great mysteries of existence (see Figure 8).

Figure 8: Coherence Through "My Personal Relationship"

However, the Kingdom of God (*God's progressive expansion of God's life-giving rule over creation, until all things are under his perfect ruling authority*) is an idea large enough to provide reasonable coherence to all the elements of life. Therefore, the **Kingdom of God is the key to understanding the whole of Scripture, and the lens through which all of life can be understood** (see Figure 9).

The Kingdom of God

Figure 9: Kingdom of God Coherence

The Kingdom of God suggests that there is a task to fulfill that is more comprehensive than "my personal relationship with God." Jesus lived, died, and rose for more than "my personal salvation." He had a <u>Throne</u> to restore and an enemy to vanquish (<u>Conquest</u>), and now he wants to continue his victorious campaign through the actions of his <u>Rescued</u> bride. Clearly, the goal of human history is to bring glory to the Son through the establishment of his Kingdom (Eph. 1.19-23).

For many years scientists have searched for what is called the Grand Unifying Theorem (GUT), which could explain everything in one giant equation. GUT is the attempt to explain what seems "unreachable, diverse, and disjunctive. It will make sense of the physical universe. The Kingdom can serve as the GUT, not just of the Bible, but of all we do, think, and are—indeed, of all existence and of all the universe."[27]

In Ephesians, Paul summed up God's "grand unifying" plan by saying he has made *"known to us the mystery of his will, according to his purpose, which he set forth in Christ as a plan for the fullness of time, to unite all things in him, things in heaven and things on earth" (Eph. 1.9-10).*

Chapter 5: The Second Cropping Tool: Rationalism

THE EFFORT TO reduce the gospel to a simpler message led to Individualism. However, there was another cultural dynamic at work that helped *crop Jesus from the picture*: **a tendency to use analytical approaches with a focus on the mind (Rationalism).**

Rationalism, a product of the Enlightenment, attempts to reduce ideas to their simplest forms. It uses logic and sequencing to organize information into systems.

Rationalism is Not A Bad Thing

The Enlightenment had a dramatic effect on the world. Centuries of analytical thinking have produced wonderful advances in medicine and technology, resulting in life-saving conveniences and improvements in the quality of life. These benefits have been among God's instruments to win back what was lost (Luke 19.10), extending blessing to people all over the earth, not just those in the developed world.

Therefore, Rationalism is not wrong or evil. However, analytical thinking is only *one way* of understanding truth.[28] One can grow in Christlike wisdom through symbol, image, experience, and intuition, not just through analytical thinking. Rationalism makes certain assumptions that are not always conducive to biblical thinking. It assumes most questions have an answer, a cause-and-effect. It sees the world as orderly and transparent, where science is equipped to de-mystify the universe. Facts are used as the means to break reality down into its component parts. The rational mind despises mystery and seeks knowledge instead. Rationalism values what can be seen and measured.

In an attempt to spread the gospel, Rationalism was employed to structure the broad Story of the Bible into simple propositional statements that would be easy for believers to memorize and communicate. In the late 1800s, helpful attempts were made to come up with lists of fundamental beliefs that Christians could affirm and communicate, such as the inerrancy of Scripture, the Virgin birth, and salvation by grace. The motivation was good, but the employment of Rationalism in these exercises had hidden implications that surfaced in later decades.

A Reasonable Faith

Rationalism suggested Christianity is reasonable, and following Christ would have the natural effect of a good life. The implication was, "those who want a good life should seek what is true and live according to truth."

Because of this assumption, Rationalism pushed believers to have logical reasons to defend their faith. It was assumed that Christianity needed to be both reasonable and relevant before others would agree with its claims. Christians were taught to value outlines, logical arguments, and propositional statements. This tended to cause believers to be defensive about their faith, especially if they felt ill-equipped to give intellectual answers to difficult questions.

The Problem of Evil

Because Rationalism seeks cause-and-effect connections, Americans have trouble understanding the existence of evil. Cultures valuing mystery over Rationalism do not struggle with the problem of evil to the extent Americans do. In fact, I have observed the effect of Rationalism, where Christians, surprised by the emergence of tragedy, expressed various versions of belief in a logical progression: "I thought if I knew the Bible, followed Christian ethical standards, and prayed, blessings would come; A+B=C. I thought the Christian life was logical, predictable, and static."

Ed Murphy said Christians believe: "if they come to Christ, life will be pleasant from then on. All will go well. God will become their divine servant. He will provide all of their needs. 'God wants to make you happy,' they are told, 'and is available to prosper you in life.' If they don't like their present job and want a better one, God will provide it. If they are sick, God will heal them. If they need a newer, more comfortable car, it is available for the asking."[29]

<u>Life Does Not Work That Way</u>

The problem with these assumptions is that life is often illogical, unpredictable, and dynamic, which is bewildering to the Rationalistic mind. Christian faith is better understood as a conflict between two kingdoms; a battle in which believers are soldiers for Christ. Rick Wood warned of people who are not told about this reality:

> There will be tremendous confusion and disillusionment when the truth of this unknown spiritual reality breaks in upon their lives. It is like a person who buys a vacation package to the French Rivera expecting a wonderful time of fun and relaxation only to discover upon his arrival that there is open warfare taking place with bombs going off,

bullets flying and the wounded littering the sandy beaches. Such a person would naturally think: "What is going on here? This is not what I signed up for."[30]

Sometimes believers cannot reconcile the inevitable trials of life, and become vulnerable to psychological problems or debilitating doubts, placing needless blame on themselves. When disaster strikes, they may lack the theological categories to deal with their pain, and without a bigger understanding of the battle between the kingdoms, the circumstances of peoples' lives can distort their view of God and his Word. With the powers of evil *cropped out of the picture*, there may be little understanding about spiritual warfare, leaving believers confused.

Francis Schaeffer said, "Though you and I have stepped from the kingdom of darkness into the kingdom of God's dear Son, we are still surrounded by a culture controlled by God's great enemy, Satan. We must live in it from the moment we accept Christ as our Savior until judgment falls. We, too, are encompassed by one who was once our king, but is now our enemy. It is just plain stupid for a Christian not to expect spiritual warfare while he lives in enemy territory."[31]

As a result of the conflict between two kingdoms, the Church is caught in cosmic crossfire. While Christians are the *object of Christ's affection*, for the devil, people are simply *objects*. The devil's aim is to hurt Christ and his causes. People are of no real interest to him. Satan desires to blind people to the truth of salvation and subject them to suffering. He *uses* people to get back at *God*. To God, people are very important, but to Satan they are simply pawns in a larger campaign.[32]

When tragedy strikes, Christians can be embittered toward God rather than realizing the source of evil is from the enemy. If God is viewed as a loving Father, who exempts his people from every source of pain and suffering, it is no wonder that many become disillusioned and leave the faith. For those oriented to Rationalism, God makes no Rationalistic sense.

But those unencumbered by the limits of Rationalism, fully aware of the dynamics of the Kingdom, can find themselves better-equipped to face trials with confidence and joy (James 1.2-4).

The Truth of the Bible

Thankfully, the Bible is not limited to Rationalistic thinking. While the Bible is always true and sometimes uses propositional statements, it is far too deep and meaningful to be constrained by *analytical approaches alone*. It *does* speak to an analytic mind, but is not limited by reason or logic.

In the Bible, not every issue has a clear answer. In fact, many questions will remain <u>unclear</u> until they will are disclosed in the future. The book of Job reveals no answers to a Rationalistic, cause-and-effect mind. God makes it clear that not all suffering is caused by the suffering person, or by anyone else, for that matter. There may be no apparent *reason* at all. Life (as interpreted by the Bible) can be deceptive and ambiguous; sacred yet mysterious; where the false masquerades as truth, and things are not always as they seem.

Rather than placing facts at the center, Scripture places the *sovereign God* at the center, with people and facts *under the rule of God*. Christ is the central player in his drama, where knowledge is only part of the grander mystery. The Bible has far fewer propositional statements than metaphor, story, symbol, or parable. Christian faith cannot be understood without images like lambs and lions, wheat and tares, sheep and goats. The Bible takes people to places that are beyond description.

Those who follow Jesus will face uncertainty, suffering, and adventure; muddled combinations of good and evil, with cosmic disorder, until he comes to set all things right. The truth of the Bible gives people the psychological means to handle hardship because Scripture does not allow the construction of clean categories where people can "figure everything out." Scripture frees believers from such foolishness. Those who try to master their world through Rationalism will end up confused and discouraged.

The Bible, especially apostolic teaching, is a witness to the unfolding Story of God in Christ. The apostles were eyewitnesses to this Story. The early Church was not so much a literate, learning community (Rationalism) as much as a "People of the Story." They preferred to hear an apostle *tell stories* about Christ rather than *study a theological paper* about him.[33]

Using Truth for Personal Gain

Robert Webber describes two approaches to Truth.[34] In the first approach people recognize Truth as objective and outside of themselves. Truth is an authority under which they joyfully submit, whether it helps them or not. This is the appropriate response to God's Word.

The second group uses Truth as a tool to *control life or make life better.* Those who use Truth for their own benefit can be characterized in two ways—**pragmatic and therapeutic:**

1. Pragmatic: "The Christian life is a perfectly rational system for life. When you accept it and live by it you will really have life by the tail. You will be able to stand up strong and face life."[35] This kind of *pragmatic* Rationalism is recognizable in many areas including evangelism training, discipleship materials, and parenting instruction. For example, drugs and sexual activity are not wrong because God said so, but because those activities are harmful and get in the way of God's best. They are not sinful, causing separation from God, but are simply detrimental to one's well-being. This leads people to look for pragmatic reasons for evaluating the rightness or wrongness of various lifestyle choices, rather than living under the authority of God's Truth.

2. Therapeutic: "What you need is an experience of Jesus Christ. When you let him come into your life and take over, you will feel much better. Everything will fall in place for you and life will be beautiful."[36] This kind of *therapeutic* Rationalism assumes a good life results from Truth. Michael Horton wrote, "Another way of saying it is that we always prefer giving God a supporting role in our life movie—our own glory story—rather than being recast in his unfolding drama of redemption. How can God fix my marriage? How can he make me a more effective leader? How can I overcome stress and manage my time and finances better?"[37]

Jesus Cropped from the Picture

These two approaches (pragmatic and therapeutic) are supported by testimonies where being a Christian has given meaning to people's lives, saved their marriages, or delivered them from an addiction. This leads to admonitions to, "Try God; give him a chance with your life. Accept him as Savior and see how your life gets better." Webber said, "I gradually began to understand that these phrases and others like them turn the gospel inside out. I once understood the gospel as God asking me to let him into my narrative, to find room for him in my heart and life. But now I realize that God bids me to find my place in his narrative."[38]

Rationalism has *cropped Jesus from the picture*, turning the gospel into a set of doctrines to be believed so life will turn out well. The next chapter will explore Rationalism's influence on the origins of a well-known, and seemingly benign phrase.

Chapter 6: How Does It Apply to Me?

RATIONALISM HELPS THE individual make personal applications that can reduce the Bible to a "guide for what I need," resulting in the ubiquitous phrase, "**How does it apply to me?**"

Analytical Approaches to Bible Study

Many Americans have been taught to focus on individual verses and chapters without reading for the larger context of Jesus' redemptive work to defeat the enemy. Instead of seeing a composite picture of the cosmic battle, Christians are too busy looking for the details to notice God's overall plan. An analytical approach to studying the Bible *crops Jesus and his purposes out of the picture.*

For example, Michael Horton explained, "Apart from Christ, the Bible is a closed book. Read with him at the center, it is the greatest story ever told. The Bible is trivialized when it is reduced to life's instruction manual. According the apostles—and Jesus himself—the Bible is an unfolding drama with Jesus Christ as its central character."[39]

Unfortunately, the purpose of Bible study is often geared to the *accumulation of information* about the Bible (information transfer). For example, if the truth were told, many Christians would confess that they find more satisfaction in *learning about* the three Greek words for love than they do in seeking to love difficult people.

These are some of the analytical approaches to Bible study:
◇ Look for verses that inspire.

⋄ Look for verses that tell what God has promised.

⋄ Look for verses that indicate God's commands.

⋄ Look for verses that will prove a particular doctrine.

⋄ Look for verses to control and/or correct others.

Frank Viola said, "Notice how each is highly individualistic. All of them put you, the individual Christian, at the center.... Each of these approaches is built on isolated proof-texting. Each treats the New Testament like a manual and blinds us to its real message."[40]

In addition, most Westerners assume that proper understanding of the Bible demands linguistic expertise or formal education, rather than the spiritual wisdom and discernment available to all the saints. This is curious, given the Reformation's emphasis on the priesthood of the believer.

For some, knowing the Bible is a source of competition and pride; a way to gain notoriety for knowing Scripture better than others. For them, "knowledge is power," and acquiring facts about the Bible can take the place of actually *knowing* Christ.

Rationalism can also leave believers thinking the Bible is boring, dry, trivial, or irrelevant, rather than allowing the Word to stir their hearts toward devotion to Christ.

The Drive for Personal Application
Christians are taught to find a direct line of application from the Bible to *Self.* The continual hunger and thirst for direct personal application to one's daily life can twist the meaning of the classic Bible study

question, "How does this apply to me?" into an exercise that makes *the reader* the SUBJECT, not Christ. Regarding this *what-does-it-say-to-you?* approach, Webber said, "Often the interpretation of well-meant personal insights is regarded as authoritative simply because 'it makes me feel good' or 'it gives me a lift.'"[41]

While it is true that there are many practical applications for daily living, the Bible was given as the Story of God's redemptive history, not as a user's guide or owner's manual. Such thinking trivializes the Scriptures and tempts the reader to skip over whole sections that "don't apply to me." For example, I have been in Bible studies on the book of Ephesians where participants were eager to skip chapters 1-3 in order to "get to the good stuff" in chapters 4-6 (where there are more practical applications).

The drive for personal application can make Christians biblically illiterate. Whether they grow up in the church or not, the inability to explain the basic plot of the biblical drama and its lead character is now no different for *churched* teens than it is for *unchurched* young people.[42]

I was a case in point. The Bible I studied in my high school days is a visual example of my bias for the most applicable parts of Scripture. I was taught to underline key verses that were especially helpful. Because the epistles were so "practical," I ended up reading and underlining them most often. Eventually, all the pages from Romans to Jude fell out. While the Gospels and Proverbs are somewhat smudged, most of the Old Testament pages remain a clean ivory color, showing they were rarely read.

Jesus Cropped from the Picture

There is little difference between this kind of neglect of the Scriptures and Thomas Jefferson's infamous attempt to "cut and paste" his own version of the Bible. Mark Batterson said, "Part of us scoffs or scolds Jefferson. You can't pick and choose. *You can't cut and paste. You can't do that to the Bible.* But here's the truth: while most of us can't imagine taking a pair of scissors to the Bible and physically cutting verses out, we do exactly what Jefferson did. We ignore verses we cannot comprehend. We avoid verses we do not like. And we rationalize verses that are too radical.... Whenever I'm reading the Bible and I come to a verse that I don't fully understand or live up to, I find myself reading really fast."[43]

I'm a New Testament Kind of Guy

Believers who say, "I am more of a New Testament kind of person" indicate they have *cropped Jesus from the picture.* Jesus is the **SUBJECT** of all of Scripture.[44] In the Old Testament God forms a family in Abraham, a tribe in Jacob, a nation in Israel, a kingdom in David. The history of the Jewish people is the story of how God prepared the world to receive the Messiah, who would fulfill all the images and prophecies of Old Testament. Jesus completes the Israelite story so the rest of the world can participate in the Hebrew's heritage.

The Old Testament is the story of Israel's expectation; the New Testament the story of Israel's fulfillment, where all creation anticipates Jesus' Second Coming, resulting in a new heaven and earth.[45]

"**How does it apply to me?**" is the question that can quench deep appreciation of God's word. The better question is, *"Why is this important to God, and why did he want it in his book?"* The proper approach to Bible study is to look for the unfolding drama of Christ's Kingdom, which may have no immediate personal application to the reader at all.

Analytical Approaches to Worship Services

When the *how-does-it-apply-to-me* attitude is extended to a local church, it becomes a personal resource center existing to "meet my needs."

Worship as Seminar

Cathy and I once attended a seminar on the differences in brain chemistry between men and women. We thought it would promote domestic tranquility and mutual understanding. I ended up learning more about contemporary approaches to worship than I did brain chemistry (although we did enjoy being together for the day).

With Cathy's experience as an audiologist, she had attended dozens of medical seminars, so she told me what to expect. There would be plenty of coffee and snacks to keep people awake. There would be warm-up jokes or exercises to get people in a learning mode. Each table would have toys to play with to keep listeners engaged. The topic would have to be interesting and the presenter sharp and entertaining, or attendees would tune out. The temperature and lighting would be maintained to create an environment conducive to learning. Finally, she said, there would be an evaluation at the end to ensure the information was presented well, and the people actually learned something they could apply in real life.

Not surprisingly, the seminar happened just as Cathy predicted. After it was over, we discussed what we had learned. We talked about the presenter, the food, the content of the seminar, and whether it had any direct application to our lives. We were happy we did not get sleepy. It passed the tests of a successful seminar.

Upon reflection, it occurred to me that the criteria Cathy and I used to evaluate our seminar are identical to the ones Americans are taught to use when evaluating a worship service:

- ⋄ An applicable topic, given by a knowledgeable and interesting presenter
- ⋄ The right learning environment, with comfortable seats, and the right room temperature
- ⋄ Warm-up activities before the teaching starts
- ⋄ *Information transfer* as the primary purpose of the event, presented in a form that could be easily remembered and applied

Using this criteria, pastors have become *seminar coordinators;* personal coaches to help people live the Christian life. Each Sunday has become a "How to Follow Jesus" seminar, where the preacher is the performer and the people are silent spectators.

Worship as Celebration

Our seminar experience made me think about what worship services *should be.* If not a seminar, what should they be? All worship gatherings should be a *celebration*, not a seminar! Worship services are for God, not the people. Jesus should be the focus of a joyous remembrance of his past victories, glorious presence, and future return.

At *celebrations*, activities are oriented around the *person being celebrated* (the guest of honor). The music, decorations, and themes are chosen *based on the guest of honor*, not the celebrators. Satisfaction comes not by each celebrator "getting something out of it," but in witnessing the joy of the person being honored.

Virtually no one would be upset if the chairs were uncomfortable, the temperature too hot, or the music not to their liking. As long as the guest of honor enjoyed the event, it would be deemed a success. There would be no expectation of an eloquent speech with direct, personal application to the celebrators' lives, because the reason for the gathering was to *extol the honored guest.*

When worship services become a *celebration* of the Story, the pastor is liberated to be an *event host* rather than a *seminar coordinator.* Jesus becomes the center of attention. The music is chosen for his benefit, not the celebrators in the pews. All the activities, including teaching, singing, communion, testimonies, and announcements are prepared with excellence *for the Lord's benefit,* not to please an audience looking for a seminar. Worship becomes a gathering to sing, tell stories of the past, hear testimonies about the present, and to look forward to a glorious future when he returns to save his people.

Every time Christians gather, they should celebrate the past, present, and future work of God.

The problem is that Christians have been trained to come to church for a seminar. They have been trained to receive a Rationalistic, structured, methodical, logical, verse-by-verse exposition of Scripture, with direct application to their lives. If the worship service does not meet their seminar expectations, they may not come back. They may choose a different church with a better seminar program, or choose to attend an adult Sunday school class and skip corporate worship altogether. Or they may sit in the pew and pray for the pastor's presentation skills to improve, just like a spectator would do at a seminar that is not very engaging, distracted by thoughts like, "our attendance would be higher if our preacher were more dynamic."

This has to disappoint the One who gave his life to deliver his flock. Although people were created to worship Christ in celebration, too often God is dishonored because his people ignore the Guest of Honor by turning services into personal-growth seminars.

Worship services are *not* occasions to re-fill listeners' spiritual tank, empowering them to head back out into the world with renewed determination. Instead, worship is a time to remember that the Church is the **OBJECT** of God's purposes (the basketball). It is a time to rediscover the Grand Story into which all people have been invited. Every time churches gather to worship Christ, they have an opportunity to "press the re-set button," to re-orient their lives around the real **SUBJECT** of the Story.

Curtis and Eldredge said that for centuries the church viewed the gospel as "a cosmic drama whose themes permeated our own stories and drew together all the random scenes in a redemptive wholeness. But our rationalistic approach to life, which has dominated Western culture for hundreds of years, has stripped us of that, leaving a faith that is barely more than mere fact-telling. Modern evangelicalism reads like an IRS 1040 form: It's all true, all the data is there, but it doesn't take your breath away."[46]

Bible study and worship services lose their impact when Jesus is *cropped from the picture.* The question, "How does this apply to me," should be replaced by, **"Why is this important to God?"**

Chapter 7: EPIC or SLIM?

IN PREVIOUS CHAPTERS, it was argued that Individualism and Rationalism are the two culprits producing boredom in the American church. In Figure 10, Individualism/Rationalism is expressed as a "**SLIM**" worldview.

A Limited World View of Christian Faith (SLIM)

Spectator-oriented (S): The posture of Christian life; primarily soaking in information, practicing personal ethics, and waiting until Jesus returns.

Linguistic (L): The message of Truth is made primarily through words, propositional statements, logic, and outlines.

Individualistic (I): The central aspect of a believer's life is "my personal relationship with Christ." The central organizing principle is personal salvation and sanctification. Christ is "my savior."

Mental (M): Truth is aimed primarily at the mind.

Figure 10: SLIM

By contrast, the Kingdom Story is expressed as an "**EPIC**"[47] worldview (see Figure 11).

A Larger View of Christian Faith (EPIC)

Experiential (E): The Truth of the Kingdom is to be experienced by the whole person (mind, will, emotions), not just the mind. *It is Mental...and more.*

Participative (P): A Christian is a representative of Christ's Kingdom work, carrying out the on-going victory over the devil's kingdom through the Church. Believers are not static spectators waiting for death, but dynamic participants in Kingdom activity. *It is Spectator...and more.*

Image-rich (I): The use of Rationalism is too limiting to be the sole means of delivering truth. Images are frequently used in the Bible and should be employed as ways to theologize, worship, disciple, and do outreach. *It is Linguistic...and more.*

Christ-centered (C): The individual is not the **SUBJECT** of Christian faith. Jesus and his Kingdom purpose is the **SUBJECT**. Christ is not only "my savior" but also "The Savior." *It includes individuals, but is primarily about Christ's Kingdom.*

Figure 11: EPIC

It is important to emphasize that various the elements of SLIM are *not wrong or heretical.* There are important spectator, linguistic, individualistic, and mental aspects of Christian faith. However, it is the **thick border** placed around SLIM that causes problems (see Figure 12). If the border is removed allowing a larger worldview, it becomes EPIC.

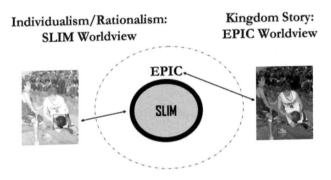

Figure 12: SLIM and EPIC Worldviews

SLIM (with a thick border) is simply too static, provincial, limited, and constraining to produce vibrant Christian faith. It does not "take your breath away." EPIC is an acrostic describing a broader, wider, more comprehensive biblical worldview, encouraging dynamic, vibrant Christian living.

Implications of SLIM

A SLIM approach can lead to unhealthy mindsets. When *my personal salvation and sanctification* becomes the key organizing principle of life, self-actualization has replaced the Lordship of Christ. Suffering becomes the primary issue to avoid, and therapy is the fall-back response to every problem. If the individual is at the center, and a counselor is trained to analyze problems using Rationalism through cause-and-effect solutions, therapy becomes a logical response to all situations. This is why America has more counselors than librarians and one-third of the world's psychiatrists.[48]

While there are many instances of mental illness where professional counseling is helpful and appropriate, most Americans do not need therapy as much as they need a *larger perspective outside themselves*. They need transcendence, not more pre-occupation with *Self*.

It has become acceptable to be narcissistic, even in the church. People are no longer ashamed to admit their narcissism. "Feeling good about yourself" is replacing the Christian's need for repentance and forgiveness for the sinful things they do.

Believers are looking deeper into themselves, or seek meaning in sports, shopping, politics, music, sex, or even church. Curtis and Eldredge said, "All of these smaller stories offer a taste of meaning, adventure, or connectedness. But none of them offer the real thing; they aren't large enough. Our loss of confidence in a larger story is the reason we demand immediate gratification. We need a sense of being alive now, for now is all we have. Without a past that was planned for us, and a future that waits for us, we are trapped in the present. There's not enough room for our souls in the present."[49]

It is no wonder people are bored. They are distracted by their own self-evaluation. When enough people adopt a SLIM mentality, a church becomes a club of nice people who meet regularly to learn more about God. The inevitable result is complacency, boredom and discouragement. *The SLIM life is a static life.*

Jesus Cropped from the Picture

Implications of EPIC

An EPIC existence is a life of perpetual opportunity. Each day promises a plethora of ways to join Christ in his effort to defeat the enemy's kingdom by doing good in the world. Christians can give a cup of cold water to someone, comfort the grieving, encourage the weak, warn the idle, persevere in midst of discouragement and pain, adopt a child, do excellent work at their jobs, serve their families by cleaning the house, provide medical care, help the poor, show mercy and compassion, set up chairs for a church meeting, share the good news of salvation, make a meal for a neighbor, listen to a hurting person without offering a solution, protect the vulnerable, advocate for the elderly or immigrant, defend people against cruel or ethnic jokes, resist temptation, provide justice in the public arena, or contend for the faith that was once for all delivered to the saints. The seemingly endless list can go on and on.

An EPIC view helps Christians see that God is at work everywhere. The Holy Spirit is busy glorifying Christ, empowering his people to do good works around the world. The Father is active in the events of history. The Son is mediating for the Church. All three persons of the Trinity are actively rebuilding what the devil destroyed. Because God is acting through the Church, relationships are restored, addictions are broken, love is expressed, lonely people experience comradery, and the brokenhearted find hope.

Accordingly, an EPIC life is a persistent and joyful engagement against all that causes pain and loss. The Church is constantly on the move, seeking to transform ugliness into something beautiful. EPIC Christians are eager to enjoy one another, welcome new people into their fellowship, and live the Spirit-filled life of love, joy, peace, patience, kindness, goodness, faithfulness, gentleness, and self-control.

An EPIC mentality helps a church operate as an army engaged in spiritual conflict, walking in step with the Holy Spirit, representing him with honor, and using freedom in Christ to be creative in outreach to the world.[50] This kind of perspective results in boldness, purpose, courage, and a sense of urgency.

How-To Video vs. Epic Story

The SLIM approach emphasizes propositional statements, outlines, and linear logic that appeal to the mind, much like a "How to Build a Deck" video purchased at Home Depot. In fact, one way to recognize a SLIM mindset is to reflect on the manner in which a person reads this very chapter. A SLIM approach would be limited to the analysis of the precise meaning of each concept, phrase, and word (Linguistic-Mental), in an attempt to arrive at Rationalistic truth.

However, an EPIC approach is not limited to outlines and logic, but employs images, metaphors, and narratives as additional ways to communicate truth, appearing much more like *The Chronicles of Narnia* than the *How-to video*. For example, an EPIC reading of this chapter would include rationalistic analysis, but would also seek to understand the big picture, and how the concepts fit into a larger scheme or narrative for the glory of God.

Categories Versus Wholeness

Because Rationalism seeks to reduce ideas to their component parts, and separate them into categories, SLIM distinguishes activities as "sacred" or "secular." By contrast, an EPIC view seeks to integrate life into a whole. Since Jesus is Lord of *all* life, Kingdom living is not limited to "religious activities," but encompasses any activity conducted as his representative.

So relaxing with friends is Kingdom living. Appreciating God's gift of a good cup of coffee is Kingdom living. Bringing a meal to a neighbor is Kingdom living. The Kingdom is about *living life under his reign*, validating his good pleasure in joy, peace, and right relationships (Rom. 14.17). **Christians can live life together as though the Kingdom were present!**

Orthodoxy Versus Orthopraxy

The primary virtues of SLIM are to <u>know</u> (Rationalism) the right doctrine and apply it in one's <u>personal</u> (Individualism) life, often with limited regard to the impact of interpersonal relationships. However, an EPIC understanding seeks to *apply doctrine* in order to be in *right relationship* with God and others. Being *rightly related* is the goal, and doctrine is a means toward that end. In other words, right belief (orthodoxy) is for the purpose of right relationship (orthopraxy).

Defensive Bible Reading

In a SLIM world, Christians must be good at apologetics, having logical answers to every question, from evolution to Postmodern thought. When I was in college, I believed this so strongly that I thought the best thing I could do for God was to get a Master's Degree in Apologetics.

I assumed the highest calling was to have answers to all the skeptics' challenges on any number of scientific, philosophical, or political issues. While having such scholarship is helpful for giving the believer confidence in the gospel, it can sometimes lead to a distorted way of viewing the Scriptures. For example, I found myself reading the Bible to prove its historic and scientific accuracy, not so much to find out the point of his Story. This is what Webber called *defensive Bible reading.*[51]

I read the Genesis creation story in a defensive way; as an account that would prove the veracity of the Bible and God's existence. The beauty of God's liturgy and vision for the world was lost on me. I was so distracted by the "when and how of creation" that I *cropped the Holy Spirit from his creation picture.* My defensive style caused me to lose the heart and soul of the Bible's message, which made the Scriptures lifeless and dry.

Instead of defensive Bible reading, believers need to be grounded in the *Story of the Kingdom*, which even young children can understand and articulate. There is no oppressive burden to be professionally educated for the purpose of convincing others, using Rationalistic arguments. Christians are free to simply present the Story clearly. The apostles were not highly educated, but they boldly reported *what they had seen.* They were eyewitnesses and ambassadors (1 John 1.1-3). Christians can do the same, releasing them from fear and defensive Bible reading.

The State of the World

A SLIM approach can also result in anxiety about the state of current affairs, while an EPIC approach concentrates on the *certainty of the*

Kingdom's triumph over every kingdom of this world (Rev. 11.15), resulting in greater peace of mind. An EPIC view produces freedom because the emphasis is on *Christ's* achievement, not the *individual's* accomplishments. Believers have victory, but it is *completely dependent on Christ.* Life is simpler when Jesus is central, but more complicated when the Self is the focus. SLIM *crops Jesus from the picture*, making the individual the **SUBJECT**. EPIC "un-crops the picture," restoring Christ as the **SUBJECT**.

Living "In Christ"

A powerful example of an EPIC view is J.R.R. Tolkein's *The Lord of the Rings,* which tells the story of a brave group of ordinary folks, called into a dangerous journey, to put an end to the evil that has overcome the world. This epic story illustrates the Christian's dependence on Christ as Champion. Two of the heroes (Merry and Pippin) are creatures called "Hobbits," who are small in stature, but passionate of heart.

Separated from their group, these Hobbits are rescued by giant living trees (Ents) who provide them with refuge from their enemies, and food to sustain them. When battle breaks out, the Hobbits throw rocks at the enemy from their protected place in the Ent treetops. The Hobbits were empowered to destroy the enemy because they were perched within the mighty Ents.

In the same way, when people are *placed* (baptized)"in Christ," they become empowered to do Kingdom work, and experience the capacity, protection, and freedom of operation only Christus Victor can provide.

Just as Merry and Pippin found shelter and sustenance through their placement (baptism) in the Ents, Christians find their source of power and refuge "in Christ." Jesus fights a battle for his people that they cannot win on their own, but because they are "in Christ," they can participate in the downfall of the enemy.

A SLIM worldview *crops Jesus from the picture*. An EPIC perspective restores Jesus to his rightful place, providing believers with purpose, good mental health, appreciation for the Bible, less anxiety about the state of the world, and a safe place from which to engage the fight of the Kingdom.

As Mark Batterson said, "He certainly didn't die on the cross to tame us. He died to make us dangerous. He died to invite us into a life of spiritual adventure."[52]

Chapter 8: Boredom and Busyness

Slim's rationalistic emphasis on separating categories into components (especially "secular versus sacred"), mixed with an erroneous view of atonement ("now that I'm saved, the work is basically done"), can result in unhealthy patterns of boredom or busyness.

Gathered and Dispersed

Each church is a community that both "gathers and disperses." Stevens said, "the church is a rhythm of gathering and dispersion, like the gathering and dispersion of blood from the heart in the human body."[53] The church gathers together for worship, fellowship, and service to one another ("inside the church"), then disperses out into the community ("outside the church").

SLIM

Under SLIM, the gap between gathered (inside) and dispersed (outside) is wide. The categories are distinct. For many, the sacred events happen *inside* (Sunday school or prayer meetings), and the secular events occur *outside* (work and recreation).

Inside is where individuals get their spiritual needs met by the church. The church is the "place" to receive what God dispenses for "my personal relationship." The number of *outside* spiritual activities is small. If there are any spiritual activities *outside*, they are often limited to personal or family devotions, which typically focus on "information transfer" (Rationalism).

Inside is where most of the opportunities for service exist, such as ushering, teaching, setting up communion, or managing the finances. These opportunities are located at the church itself (*inside*), and are done by a few specialists who have the greatest competence to carry them out. The few ministry activities that take place *outside* are often delegated to paid clergy or missionaries.

The *inside* time investment is typically limited to three hours on a Sunday morning, two hours for a mid-week study or small group, and an hour of some other mid-week volunteer work at the church. Christians picture themselves "going to church" (*inside*), and "living life" (*outside*).

Some people find this routine <u>boring</u> because they "punch the clock" each week, checking off their duties. However, the <u>busy</u> person finds the routine guilt-producing because there is always more that could be done: "I should do more at church; I should read my Bible and pray more; I should share my faith more." Life becomes overwhelming because there is never enough time to fulfill their spiritual duties.

EPIC

While the *inside* and *outside* categories can be helpful, an EPIC perspective seeks to blur these distinctions, where Christians see themselves as ambassadors that represent Christ wherever they go, knowing their local congregation is "the agent of the Kingdom" in their community. This presents a wider array of ministry opportunities through work, leisure, hobbies, and relationships.

For example, the Kingdom is advanced when a husband lovingly listens to his wife, a politician does her job with integrity, a school teacher upgrades his curriculum, a mother welcomes her children after school, a neighbor plays checkers with an elderly shut-in, or a stockbroker offers wise counsel. All these activities represent a King who wants to win back that which was lost to the enemy (Luke 19.10).

These actions extend beyond what are normally considered "spiritual," encompassing every aspect of life. By definition, all waking hours are spent in ministry. The question is not whether people are *ministering* or not; the only question is whether they are ministering *well* or not.

Bob Roberts describes the EPIC life when he challenges believers to be *totally wild spirits*, who seek to do more than live the "inside" kind of faith. "It's fun to live the Christian life in such a way that you don't always know the next bend or how the current bend is going to impact you. When you live life on pilgrimage, you are learning to walk by faith, something we don't do a lot of today."[54]

This kind of walk empowers Christians to realize they can make a difference every moment of the day. They can do things they never dreamed possible, living in a sense of adventure and risk, which is what following God is all about. Church members can be free from the limitations of religious work on Sunday alone, recognizing that their service is from "sunup to sundown." God is at work in their families and their relationships, making all of life sacred. The results of this outlook are companionship, unity, maturity, and meaning.

In addition, EPIC Christians can see their vocation as their number one ministry, not just a way to make a living. Those who gain this perspective, seeing themselves as agents of the Kingdom, will care for people in workplaces that historically have not been thought of as Kingdom locations. A believer's presence *brings the Kingdom into it.*

The Bored

An EPIC perspective changes bored people into totally wild spirits, whose lives are characterized by *new opportunities.* Boredom is a sign of *cropping Jesus from the picture*; of compartmentalizing life in the secular versus sacred; the *inside* versus *outside.* Bored Christians have made *their personal fulfillment* the SUBJECT.

Because of this, the bored are not "free in Christ" because they are dependent on diversions. They need relationships or activities that provide meaning and comfort, such as recreation, entertainment, shopping, or food. Freedom in Christ means believers are encouraged to enjoy all good things without guilt, but are content with, *or without* such diversions. Since all their needs are met in Christ, they are free to *enjoy* recreation or food, without being *dependent* upon them. Such diversions are neither evil *nor* important.

The Busy

An EPIC view can free busy, burned-out, overworked believers from fulfilling their duty through "spiritual activities." Guilt is probably a sign of taking on more than God intends, living under the law rather than by grace. "Busy" people are not *free in Christ* because they depend on their own performance to provide meaning or comfort. Freedom in Christ means believers are free to work hard for Christ, but are content by being "in Christ." Their contentment is not based on their achievements.

When *Self* becomes the center, dangers result. As Stevens said, "Boredom and busyness are symptoms of the same disease of self-centeredness. People who are either compulsively busy or chronically bored do not have God at the center."[55]

When *Jesus is cropped from the picture*, boredom and busyness are not far behind.

Chapter 9: I Don't Feel Fed!

WHENEVER I HEAR, "I don't feel fed," I immediately suspect Individualism and Rationalism ("I"=self and "fed"=knowledge).

However, drawing such a conclusion can be premature. For example, Jesus instructed Peter to "feed my sheep" (John 21.17) and there *is* a biblical basis for making sure the flock receives knowledge (2 Pet. 1.5-6). If the sheep claim to be hungry, shepherds should pay attention. Believers need a steady diet of teaching from the Word to grow in their love for God and to stay healthy for God's Kingdom work. So leaders who neglect this responsibility do their congregations a disservice.

But often there is something more behind the statement, "I don't feel fed." What people are often saying is they are not getting the *kind* of *knowledge* they want. While it is possible their pastors are not giving them nutritious food from the Bible, in a SLIM world it is just as likely that *they are picky eaters.*

Children who receive healthy food from their parents might refuse it in preference for their favorite foods—or junk food. Pastors face the same dilemma. Rather than focusing on consistent exposure to the whole of God's Word, preachers are pressured to feed the flock *in a certain way so that it meets the listener's personal needs.*

To make matters worse, sometimes people make mutually exclusive requests. For example, some want expositional teaching, others more topical; some want practical application and others want deeper theology. There can be requests for more interactive discussion rather than the traditional "man on the elevated platform." Everyone wants the information presented in an interesting way so they can apply it easily (see Chapter 6, "Worship as Seminar").

Unfortunately, in a SLIM environment, where the individual is at the center, a pastor is constantly under pressure to meet the *individual's needs*, whether it is good for the church or not. Frost and Hirsch said, "It's very hard to have a prophetic ministry to the group that provides your salary ... Leadership is thus always hostage to the reactionary groups in the congregation."[56]

An Expected Pattern

A SLIM orientation expects a *certain kind of preaching* that "charges me up to get through the next week." When this expectation is not met, the person leaves deflated, like the feeling one has after watching a disappointing movie or witnessing the defeat of a favorite athletic team.

For this kind of listener, many sermons can be preached without much taking root in their life. Frank Viola says, "The sermon acts like a momentary stimulant. Its effects are often short-lived. Let's be honest. There are scores of Christians who have been sermonized for decades, and they are still babes in Christ."[57] People like this come to church for feeding and leave feeling depleted. Over time a pattern develops: expectation, disappointment; expectation, disappointment.

SLIM Christians have been oriented to this pattern, and if it happens long enough, they will inevitably leave their church and go to another church where their needs are met. Or they may attempt to fulfill their needs from a small group or media teaching, avoiding the worship service altogether. When the new church or small group no longer meets their needs, they find another church (this is one reason "church-hopping" is normal in America). Or they may stop going to church entirely.

The Young and the Old

I have observed this self-orientation ("I don't feel fed") intensify in recent years. For example, I have heard young people say they will not go to church because "it is boring." Their parents are quick to agree and do not challenge their children's assumptions. I have seen teenagers given the freedom to walk the streets while their parents worship, a visible sign that parents and teens agree that church must "meet my needs." Christ is *cropped from their picture.*

However, young people can be brought off the streets and into the adult life of the church. Teens have more capacity for adult faith than they are given credit for and are ready to be challenged to do great things for God. Their feelings of boredom are an indicator of how little they comprehend the wonder of the Kingdom of God and the low level of confidence adults have in their teens' abilities.

Senior citizens fall into the same self-oriented trap when they say, "we pay the bills around here." They *crop Jesus from the picture* when they threaten to stop giving unless their demands for songs or preaching style are met. Like young people, senior citizens need to be viewed as productive servants, not left to languish in a state of spiritual retirement.

Jesus Cropped from the Picture

<u>Worship Wars</u>

The inevitable result of this pre-occupation with "feeling fed" is known as "worship wars," where divisions are drawn over the styles of music that are most meaningful to various groups. No longer are Christ's interests the central issue, but how many choruses should be sung versus traditional hymns. Conversations after the service are about whether or not the worship leader chose "the good songs."

I remember singing a worship song in church, when a gentleman turned around to me and made a lengthy diatribe about the style and volume of the music. I was stunned that he would interrupt such a sacred moment and finally I said, "I am trying to worship Jesus here, can we talk about this later?"

In this environment, Christ is no longer the SUBJECT *of worship*. He has been *cropped from his own celebration*. Instead, the primary discussion is about the length of the sermon or what kind of props, videos, or skits will make it interesting so everyone can be satisfied. The typical questions in this environment are, "Did you get anything out of the sermon? How did the preacher do? Were the songs uplifting? Was communion meaningful for you?" These are SLIM questions.

<u>Attendance Is Not the Measure</u>

When people are dissatisfied with the style of preaching or the lack of programs to meet their needs, church leaders fear that attendance may decrease. Diminishing attendance can be the pastor's greatest fear because it is the primary measure of pastoral effectiveness. Jethani said, "The assumption is that with the right curriculum, the right principles, and the right programs God's Spirit will act to produce the outcomes we desire. This plug-and-play approach to the Christian life makes God a cosmic vending machine, and it assumes his Spirit resides within well-produced organizations and systems rather than people."[58]

However, *there is no biblical correlation between effective leadership and church attendance.* A pastor-teacher may be offering excellent feeding to the flock, but attendance could be *declining*. A quick overview of the Bible proves that a leader's obedience to God sometimes means *fewer* followers, not more. Sometimes Paul is worshiped as a Greek god (Acts 14.11), and other times he has to be lowered in a basket to avoid being killed (Acts 9.25). The same person can have a growing ministry in one town and has to escape for his life in another. Even Jesus had occasions where his ministry declined in numbers (John 6.66). There are no guarantees that numerical growth will automatically come from effective church leadership.

Happily, an EPIC perspective frees leaders from having to meet the felt-needs of the flock. Instead, pastors can turn their attention to preaching about *Christ and his Kingdom,* telling the Story of his acts of deliverance throughout history, which expands the congregation's capacity for love and service. Pastors can remind the flock that "his Story has met our story" and that each individual is invited into the cosmic drama revealed in his Word.

Preaching can focus on the past, present, and future victories won by the Lord Jesus. Every element of the worship service can be oriented around Christ rather than the individual (see Appendix 4), freeing pastors to spend more energy equipping the saints for the work of ministry (Eph. 4.11-13).

Also, those who are liberated from the tyranny of being "picky eaters" will find new levels of depth in Christ. "I don't feel fed" will be replaced by, "I have never been so full!" SLIM questions can be replaced by EPIC exclamations: "We experienced God together. God became so much bigger to me—I forgot that his Kingdom does not begin and end with me. I feel more prepared to live for the sake of others!"

This perspective gives hymns and choruses a new meaning because they are sung for the King, not for personal fulfillment. As Christ becomes central, preaching and music styles become secondary. Communion becomes a reminder of the coming King, who waits to share it with his Bride in the Kingdom fulfilled (Mark 14.25), not just a reminder of his death on the cross *for me*.

Pastoral Burnout

Keeping everyone happy and "feeling fed" is an impossible task. It is no wonder so many pastors burn out and leave the ministry. In many cases they are expected to be moral giants, fun to be with, open and available to everyone at all times, world-class presenters, excellent administrators, and insightful counselors.[59] In a therapeutic and entertainment-crazed culture, they are asked to do an impossible job, carrying a load that God never intended. Pastors of SLIM churches are dazed and confused about the purpose of the church, and they often feel guilty for their personal shortcomings.

However, when church leaders view the church as the agent of the Kingdom, and mobilize the church as an outpost, they equip the saints for the work of Christ in the world. The natural result is refreshment, joy, and zeal.

Pastors who realize a SLIM environment demoralizes themselves and their flock should refuse to reside there despite the pressure to do so. When *Jesus is restored to the picture*, pastors can be refreshed and the sheep can feel fed.

Chapter 10: This Is Not Working for Me

ANOTHER RESULT OF the SLIM life is that it leaves people feeling unfulfilled.

One reason for this is that church life is a complicated web of social taboos and lingo that make it difficult for newcomers to penetrate.[60] Church culture can be difficult to grasp. What people need is a simple, bottom-line, easy-to-understand philosophy of life.

Instead, they are introduced to a dizzying array of ideas, delivered through books and media, each vying for their attention. Every option must be evaluated for its relative usefulness to the individual's walk with God, in order to discover "God's plan for their life." They are promised that God has a "prosperous future and a hope" for them, but the *pressure is on* to find their personal gifts, their call, and their place in life.

Without this discovery, they fear life will not be fulfilling. But there are so many competing voices, so many choices, so many opportunities, that it is nearly impossible to make sense of it all. When the *Self* becomes the **SUBJECT**, it overwhelms most people. They are left to navigate their *own* spirituality. They feel alone.

By contrast, an EPIC approach, with Christ and his Kingdom at the center, provides a clean and simple way to incorporate new believers amongst the cacophony of competing voices. Theology becomes a means of knowing the person of Jesus Christ, not fulfilling one's life.

Ministry becomes an expression of God's ultimate purposes, lived out in daily life. Christians can find peace by allowing God to guide them in light of his *plan for the ages*, rather than straining to discover a *personalized plan for their lives*. All of an individual's life can then be oriented around a single theme: **God's work to progressively destroy the devil's kingdom through Jesus Christ.**

This theme provides every individual believer with a lifelong Kingdom task, but without the anxiety of accomplishing it alone. Dr. Don Davis likes to describe the enormity of the Kingdom by comparing believers to a lady bug, on a leaf, floating down the Amazon. His point is that while individual work on the leaf is important, most of the activity is achieved by the *movement of the river*. The immensity of God's Kingdom grants believers comfort and security because he does the "heavy lifting."

<u>Finding Meaning</u>
David Wells summarized the work of Reinhold Niebuhr, who said that throughout history individuals have found meaning through <u>family</u>, <u>community</u>, and <u>craft</u>.[61] Until recently, nearly everyone had a stable family, lived in community, and was fairly certain what their lifelong job (craft) would be. They could spend their lifetime honing their skills as a "butcher, baker, or candlestick maker."

Unfortunately, in America there has been a meltdown of the nuclear <u>family</u>, and <u>community</u> has been replaced by globalization and flat networks (often found in electronic media). Also, the industrial revolution demolished most opportunities for a lifetime <u>craft</u>. Without *family, community,* and *craft,* individuals are now left to form their *own* personal meaning. In a church, a SLIM approach only reinforces these problems, leaving people lonely and unfulfilled, continually seeking personalized adventure and meaning. However, an EPIC approach helps a person find Niebuhr's categories of *family, community,* and *craft* through the Kingdom of God.

Family can be found in the life of the local church. "One is not subjected to an individualistic salvation, in which one stands alone, but is introduced to a community of people who provide social, moral, and psychological assistance to the converting person undergoing a radical change in life."[62]

Community is experienced within the universal Church (the past, present, future people of God, across all cultures). Each local church can be traced back through its history to the first Church at Pentecost. That first Church found its roots in the nation of Israel, which is connected back through the generations to Adam and Eve, who were created in the image of the Triune God, who is the Eternal Community that has been self-existent from ages past. When people understand they are a part of God's "set-apart community," they can find the meaning and identity Niebuhr describes.

Craft is practiced through the individual's contribution to Christ's Kingdom by use of their spiritual gifts. Each person has a job to do within a local church, endowed by the Spirit to make their contribution to the Kingdom's task. An EPIC view provides people with destiny, purpose, and meaning because the Kingdom provides them with a *family, community, and craft.*

Jesus Cropped from the Picture

A Wartime Footing or Peacetime Mentality?

The final reason people feel unfulfilled is because they approach the Christian life as *peacetime soldiers*. Soldiers have more accidents and get in more interpersonal conflict during peacetime than they do during times of war. Life is difficult in wartime, but monotonous in peace. I experienced a dramatic contrast between a *Peacetime Mentality* and a *Wartime Footing* when the Rodney King verdict was announced in 1992.

I was only blocks away when the Los Angeles Riots erupted at Florence and Normandie. I remember mobs of looters forming, fires breaking out, and fearing for my life as I drove the 12 miles north to my home from South Central Los Angeles. As I pulled off the interstate, I breathed a sigh of relief.

Still shaken, I turned a corner and saw a man casually hosing off his sidewalk, smoking a cigar. I felt the urge to pull over and angrily shout at the man, "Don't you know there is a riot breaking out?! People are dying, looters are ransacking businesses, and the city is being destroyed! Don't you care?" Then I realized, he had no personal experience with the danger I had just encountered. For him, it was just another sunny day in Southern California.

The reaction of this man is much like American Christians today. Peacetime Christians have no existential sense of the spiritual danger all around them. They do not feel the persistent war between the two kingdoms that is so tangible to the rest of the world. A calm suburban environment can lull SLIM Christians to sleep. When tragedy hits, they may be shocked to re-discover the spiritual battle that was present all along, feeling ill-prepared to handle it.

Peacetime in the Military
Without a common enemy, peacetime soldiers fight over trivial matters, often resenting one another. With a focus on self, complaints about the conditions of quarters, food, and command structure abound. There is stifling boredom and a longing for excitement. Without an outlet for innovation, creativity languishes. The longer soldiers live in peacetime, the deeper their roots go, making it difficult to deploy them to another assignment.

In the church, peacetime Christians fight over trivial matters. They complain about the pastor, the preaching, the programs, or the comfort of the pews. If revival broke out in Libya and the elders asked for volunteers to go and strengthen the church there, most people would have roots that go so deep, they could not imagine giving up their lifestyle to leave home, even for a short time.

Wartime
Soldiers with a *wartime footing* have no time for fighting over trivia. Their identity is found in the group they represent, having a respect for the chain of command. They work hard to develop their skills so they can contribute to their unit, not for personal achievement. Because of their dangerous wartime environment, they innovate with dramatic creativity. They are vigilant, watching for surprises from the enemy, never assuming they are competent enough to act alone. They are ready to serve at a moment's notice, and always available for re-deployment.

For Christians who have suffered, especially those who live in poverty, it is no surprise that life is hard, tragedy strikes often, and encounters with evil are a daily part of life. Believers who live outside America's middle class (which is most of the world's population) know by experience that a *wartime footing* is the <u>only</u> way to live the Christian life.

Peacetime Distractions

Part of the reason Christians struggle with so many sinful addictions and distractions is because they live like peacetime soldiers. Mark Batterson said, "One reason many of us get entangled in sin is because we don't have enough God-ordained vision to keep us busy. The more vision you have, the less you will sin. And the less vision you have the more you will sin. It is a vision from God that keeps us playing offense spiritually. Too often we try to stop sinning by not sinning ... The way to stop sinning is not by focusing on not sinning. The way to stop sinning is by getting a God-sized vision that consumes all your time and energy."[63]

A God-sized vision gives EPIC Christians a *wartime footing.* They have no time for meaningless arguments and are fiercely loyal to their leaders and co-laborers. Concentrating less on themselves and more on their contribution to the Kingdom, they work hard at the spiritual disciplines and seek creative ways to represent Christ inside and outside the church. They seek to learn more about God, but never assume they have everything figured out. They are willing to be surprised by God, but never caught off guard by the enemy's schemes.

John White said, "It need not surprise us that as an image to convey the nature of Christian living, the Holy Spirit uses that of warfare. No image could be more apt. The same courage, the same watchfulness, loyalty, endurance, resourcefulness, strength, skill, knowledge of the enemy, the same undying resolve to fight to the end come what may and at whatever cost *must* characterize Christian living as they do earthly warfare.... *To acknowledge Jesus as Savior and Lord is to join an army. Whether you know it or not, you have enlisted.*"[64]

Why So Much War Talk?

In a violent and war-torn world, many people prefer to avoid the language of warfare. Also, because evil actions like crusades, witch hunts, and inquisitions have been associated with Christianity, believers naturally desire to distance themselves from such aggressive terminology. They struggle with the emphasis on soldiering, preferring other biblical metaphors about sheep and pastures, easy yokes, and light burdens.

Because the nature of God's Kingdom is beyond full understanding, God provides a *variety of metaphors* in the Bible. God is both Warrior *and* Shepherd, King *and* Servant, Lion *and* Lamb. To approach even an elementary understanding of God's ways, believers need the cumulative effect of *all* the richness of *every* biblical metaphor.

These images break down if taken by themselves, juxtaposed against each other. "Am I a sheep or a soldier?" is the wrong question. Christians are sheep *and* soldiers, creatures which have much in common. For example, sheep and soldiers have mortal enemies and are dependent on their leaders for survival and direction. Also, sheep and soldiers function in groups (flocks and platoons).

But there are differences as well. God cares for his sheep, tenderly nursing them back to health when they are downtrodden and discouraged. His heart for the poor, marginalized, and broken is one reason there are so many comforting images of "shepherds" and "still waters" (James 2.5, Luke 4.18, Isa. 61.1-4). If there were only military metaphors, believers might be tempted to screen out the weak, like those "looking for a few good men."

The Church is not comprised of an exclusive, elite guard of Navy Seals. It is a family that welcomes the lowest, weakest, and most vulnerable. Even children are at the top of the Kingdom's priorities (Matt. 18.4). So while believers are soldiers, they also treasure the weakest among them. No one is expendable.

While God cares for people at their lowest, his desire is to transform the weak so they are strong. His grace is made perfect in weakness (2 Cor. 12.9), so people can fight the good fight of faith (1 Tim. 6.12), but not in the fleshly way of the world (2 Cor. 10.4). The Church engages the world, the flesh, and the devil through the power of the Holy Spirit, as they love and forgive one another, gently displaying all the fruit of the Spirit (Gal. 5.22-23).

When Jesus is *cropped from the picture*, Christians lose their wartime footing and become confused about their purpose. The SLIM life is one that "is not working for me." The EPIC life, though difficult, is full of meaning and purpose.

Chapter 11: The SLIMming Effect

THE SLIM LIFE is a narrow, self-oriented, and provincial life that leads to arrested development. Consider how new believers are often introduced to life in Christ.

First, they are oriented to an American church sub-culture designed for individual Christlike maturity, characterized by "your new personal relationship with Christ." Often this involves a list of ethics ("we do *this*, we do not do *that*"). Each church has its own "list," although it may be unspoken. The list might address personal morality (like dating policies), doctrine (a mode of baptism), or politics (favoring one political party over the other). Over time, the new believer discovers which activities are respected (like daily Bible study) and which ones are frowned upon (perhaps watching R-rated movies).

After being initiated into this sub-culture, a person knows which ethical, doctrinal, and political beliefs are expected. The person then begins a lifelong effort to become proficient in those same ethical, doctrinal, and political activities. The goal is *know more and do more*, but only within the activities approved on "the list."

This emphasis leads to an increasingly narrow life that eliminates much of the adventure of the Christian life, which I call the "SLIMming Effect." The *SLIMming Effect* slowly domesticates intrepid soldiers for Christ until they feel like robots living in a cage of monotonous routine.

Jesus Cropped from the Picture

Moralism, Factualism, Particularism

Robert Webber argued that what I call the *SLIMming Effect* comes from three sources: moralism, factualism, and failure to see things holistically (particularism).[65]

Moralism

Believers are taught to understand the Bible by searching for *moral examples*. For instance, when children are taught the story of Abraham, his faith in God is highlighted as he offered to sacrifice Isaac, or his moral failure is pointed out when he fathered Ishmael with Hagar. Either principle provides a practical application to daily living. There is little attention paid to Abraham as an object in the overall *Story of God's redemption,* because the plot of the Story does not provide a useful <u>moral</u> for the individual Christian to apply.

Michael Horton said, "How often have we heard the Old Testament interpreted as a collection of pious stories that we can use for our daily life? From Genesis we might have any number of heroes to imitate and villains to shun. I never knew growing up in evangelicalism that the Old Testament was about Christ. I thought it was about Bible heroes whose character I was to emulate.... Given the moralistic expectations often assumed it is no wonder that people find the Old Testament boring and much of the New Testament incomprehensible."[66]

Factualism

Rationalism prizes the accumulation of *facts over wisdom*. As a result, Christians are taught to store up information, and construct doctrinal systems where that information can be housed. This is why some people value expositional preaching, because it has a steady stream of information, but it frequently lacks connection of facts to the overall Story.

An example of *factualism* is the SLIM approach to the study of end times (eschatology). *Jesus' Story is cropped out of the picture* by making eschatology a mental exercise (Rationalism) to figure out "when Christ would come to rescue me" (Individualism), rather than how "Christ would overthrow the powers of evil and take his rightful place on the throne." Eschatology becomes less about the *exaltation of Christ* and more about *what Christ could do for the individual.*

Particularism

The Rationalistic impulse to break the whole into component parts for further analysis is *particularism*. This analytical approach has produced profound blessings through medical and technological advances, and also provided helpful biblical scholarship for the Church. The separation of the Bible into chapters and verses is an example.

But the tendency to break the Story into smaller categories has had a deleterious effect. Christians are taught to use these techniques by reading the Bible verse by verse, word by word, syllable by syllable, breaking it down to the smallest degree so the meaning can be micro-analyzed. Rarely is there a connection back to the overall context of the Story of God's redemption (Kingdom of God), leaving believers deprived of a global perspective.

Christians often receive a series of fragmented thoughts that have no connecting point beyond their personal experience. Those who take in information primarily for their individual consumption can become distracted by learning facts, growing stagnant in their capacity to represent Christ.

Children's programs emphasizing rote Scripture memory, without any connection to the biblical Story, exemplify *particularism*. A better approach is to help children not only memorize verses, but also learn their connection to the Bible's over-arching Story.

Moralism emphasizes ethics, factualism prizes knowledge, and particularism miniaturizes a believer's outlook on life. When these are combined, they produce the *SLIMming Effect,* a life that is too predictable and lacking adventure, where the desire to take risks for Christ diminishes over time. The *SLIMming Effect* results in arrested development.

However, some Christians are comfortable with a safe, predictable, and easy routine. They do not find the SLIM life constraining, and actually *prefer* "this provincial life." Curtis and Eldredge said it this way:

> Part of us would rather return to Scripture memorization, or Bible Study, or service—anything that would save us from the unknowns of walking with God.... The choice before us now is to journey or to homestead, to live like Abraham the friend of God, or like Robinson Crusoe, the lost soul cobbling together some sort of existence with whatever he can salvage from the wreckage of the world. Crusoe was no pilgrim; he was a survivor, hunkered down for the duration. He lived in a

very, very small world where he was the lead character and all else found its focus in him. Of course, to be fair, Crusoe was stranded on an island with little hope of rescue. We *have* been rescued, but still the choice is ours to stay in our small stories, clutching our household gods and false lovers, or to run in search of life. [67]

A Prison Called "SLIM"

For those who feel imprisoned by the *SLIMming Effect*, there are three means of escape.

The First Means of Escape

The most common method of escape is what Dr. Don Davis calls "Substitute Centers to a Christ-Centered Vision" (See Figure 13).

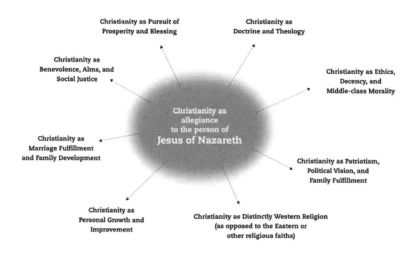

Substitute Centers to a Christ-Centered Vision
Goods and Effects Which Our Culture Substitutes as the Ultimate Concern
Rev. Dr. Don L. Davis

Christianity as Pursuit of Prosperity and Blessing

Christianity as Doctrine and Theology

Christianity as Benevolence, Alms, and Social Justice

Christianity as Ethics, Decency, and Middle-class Morality

Christianity as allegiance to the person of Jesus of Nazareth

Christianity as Marriage Fulfillment and Family Development

Christianity as Patriotism, Political Vision, and Family Fulfillment

Christianity as Personal Growth and Improvement

Christianity as Distinctly Western Religion (as opposed to the Eastern or other religious faiths)

Figure 13: Substitute Centers

Jesus Cropped from the Picture

As the SLIM prison walls creep in, a person empowered by the Holy Spirit desires to break out of the constraints and find a positive outlet for their energy. *Substitute Centers* are good things; but they are *ends in themselves*, distracting people from the main point of the Story.

For example, some latch on to doctrinal and theological issues, spending enormous energy to get others to agree with their views. Others make eschatology their life's passion, trying to determine times and dates the Lord specifically said would not be revealed (Matt. 24.36). Ethical, political, or moral causes (liberal or conservative) become an outlet for many, while others entrench themselves in marriage and family fulfillment.

Substitute Centers explain why American Christians have a voracious appetite for the *new and novel*; the latest book, seminar or fad. There have been "40 Days" of everything, Promise Keepers, small-groups, the prayer of Jabez, and the newest book or Bible study by popular authors. They are typically pursued with great zeal and quickly forgotten, leaving people hopeful that the next *Substitute Center* will fill their needs. None of them is wrong by themselves, but the manic pursuit of the next exciting development indicates an unhealthy dependence on the *new and novel*.

This is one reason for the proliferation of books on various topics like marriage and family, eschatology, health and wellness, and personal finance. All of these topics are useful, but when they substitute for *Christ and his Kingdom Story*, and become the latest craze, they can be counter-productive, *cropping Jesus from the picture.*

Regardless of the *Substitute Center*, some who *crop Jesus from the picture* in this way eventually burn out, no longer finding fulfillment in their pursuit. They find themselves back in the same SLIM prison, seeking a new *Substitute Center* to replace the previous one, repeating the cycle of frustration (see Figure 14).

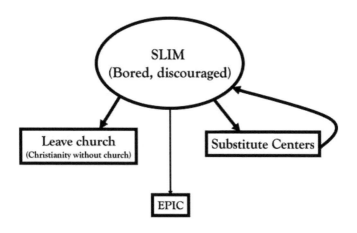

Figure 14: A Prison Called SLIM

The Second Means of Escape

The second way to escape the SLIM prison is to leave the aggravations of church and attempt to be a Christian without church, an increasingly common response according to Barna's *Revolution*. Such people have been deceived to think that Christianity is about "me and my personal relationship," failing to see their role is to join Christ in his work to destroy the work of the devil through the Church. Unfortunately, except under rare circumstances, there is no Christianity outside of the Church (see Chapter 3). Separated from a local body, these refugees may further *crop Jesus from the picture* by becoming increasingly self-absorbed.

Jesus Cropped from the Picture

The Best Means of Escape

Neither *Substitute Centers* nor *Christianity without church* provide lasting freedom from a SLIM prison. The best way to escape is to move to a bigger abode, from *me and my personal relationship* (SLIM), to *Christ and his Kingdom* (EPIC). Freedom in Christ provides a new *identity*, centered on Christ's interests in his cosmic Story.

This EPIC identity introduces a new Christian into the Kingdom of God, not a particular ethical, doctrinal, or political sub-culture. New believers find they are part of something that pre-dates them or their local church, a heritage that is ancient, and will go on after they die. *The Story* is primary, not ethics, doctrine, or political views. The goal of Christian faith is not personal growth, blessing, or self-improvement. It is something much more majestic and transcendent; a Story larger than their morals, their church, or their country.

The majesty of this perspective releases believers to ever-expanding possibilities toward a purpose greater than themselves. There can be joy in suffering for the good of Christ's Kingdom, and a growing concern for the welfare of others. EPIC is the best means of escape from the *SLIMming Effect.*

Christians do not need the latest trend, the hippest approach, or the freshest idea. What is needed is a return to the old, old Story that has been there all along. As Hauerwas and Willimon said, "Salvation is baptism into a community that has so truthful a story that we forget ourselves and our anxieties long enough to become part of that story, a story God has told in Scripture and continues to tell in Israel and the church."[68]

The *SLIMming Effect* **promotes arrested development, but an EPIC perspective provides opportunity for growth.**

I know this is true because I have seen it in the people around me. I have been amazed to see the effects of the Story on my son Ryan. When he was 16, he blogged the following on his MySpace and later shared it as a testimony before the congregation:

> Stories have always been a huge part my life. When I was little, I was fascinated with stories like Star Wars, ok mostly Star Wars, but what kindergarten boy wasn't? I loved those movies to death, never really enjoying them for their great story or characters, only space battles and lightsaber fights. When those had become a part of my past, I learned to read. Oh, this was a moment that expanded my possibilities exponentially. I read books on everything, war, romance, adventure, sci-fi; you name it I read it. I continued to read and watch movies until I was like 10, expanding my literary palette every year. Soon, I began to look at all kinds of stories trying to find deeper meanings and using them to escape. The ones I liked the most were adventure stories, where the main character is thrust into a difficult situation, and is forced to grow up really fast, and become a hero (that's because I always wanted it to happen to me). Right before the end of my eighth grade year, my parents asked me if I wanted to go through a process to symbolize and confirm my faith in Christ. At first, I only said yes because I felt it was important, not fully knowing how life-changing it was going to be. I was required to read the book, *Epic*,[69] and

do several studies of the Bible. Once I had completed these tasks I would have a ceremony with all of the influential people in my life to celebrate my commitment. One of the things I had to do as part of the study was to tell the story of the Bible in under a minute. This got the wheels turning. Like most kids my age, I had never thought about it before, and I was required to look it up. The more I did, the more intrigued I was with it. I found that most of the greatest elements in a story happened to be in God's story as well. The more I found these, the more fascinated I became with God's storytelling abilities. Rebellion, war, new life, huge mistakes, new hope, chosen people, chosen one, friendship, betrayal, sacrifice, galactic conflict, return of a king, and a battle to end all evil, were the main themes. I began to notice many of these concepts in some of my favorite books and movies (yes Star Wars included). I realized that was why I loved stories and storytelling so much because we are in the midst of the most epic, amazing story ever told. I also realized, I had become a character in this story, thrust into a difficult situation where I can't afford to not grow up fast and become a hero. My secret wish had come true. I was no longer an average kid living an average life. I was a warrior, fighting for my army, and destroying evil on a daily basis. Suddenly, my life became much more thrilling, not to mention it made way more sense. Now I realized that all aspects of my life are part of God's story that he chose to tell through me. As someone who loved these kinds of things to begin with, it was indescribably incredible to become part of the Greatest Story Ever Told.

Conclusion

The journey that began in Wichita with Brian, that continued when I heard Belle cry out for freedom from "this provincial life," came to partial conclusion when I realized **the SLIM life is the provincial life**. SLIM has produces bored, overbusy, confused, malnourished, distracted, and discouraged Christians in frequent need of therapy, many of whom have left the church in frustration.

This should be a warning to every Christian, because the temptation to *crop Jesus from the picture* is present in every church. For example, any faith tradition can emphasize a doctrine, social issue, project, or controversy which then becomes the newest cause to champion. While there is freedom in Christ to engage any number of important topics, nothing should supplant the Kingdom of God as the primary purpose for which we live. Acknowledgment of the Lordship of Jesus must always take priority over any other concern, as important as each one might be.

Despite such temptations, my observation is that Christians do not remain motivated by doctrine, liturgies, causes, the latest fad or seminar, or anything else that can c*rop Jesus from the picture*. For centuries, believers have been animated by **the ancient Story of a King, who rescued his Bride from the clutches of an evil oppressor, and is now working to put that enemy down forever, by empowering his people to be the agency of his own victory.**

Through the ages, this existential reality has moved his followers to great heights, giving them a reason to stand up and cheer; to sing his praises; to love, serve, give, and suffer for his sake. Thanks be to

God, every believer can be released to represent the King, follow his commands, and experience a foretaste of the Kingdom to come!

Like Belle, believers are longing for adventure. Happily, it exists in the epic Story of Christus Victor. There *is* more than "this provincial life."

However, my journey was not done. While I understood more about the problem, I needed to know how I got so far off track. How did I *crop Jesus from the picture*? **Part Two** (Do You Know Where You're Going To?) chronicles the next phase of my quest.

⛌

Jesus, have mercy on us. We have sinned by cropping you from your own Story. We have inserted ourselves in your rightful place and made you the object of our own personal story. Help us see ourselves in proper perspective again.

Part Two: Do You Know Where You're Going To?

"Do you know where you're going to?

- Diana Ross

....

The system producing bored Christians was formed by the blending of American marketing principles and the good intentions of believers seeking to advance the cause of Christ. This system took shape in three methods, each seeking to re-invigorate the church: Traditional, Pragmatic, and Emerging.

Chapter 12: SLIM's Shaping Forces

THE YEAR 1975 was a pivotal year in my life. I graduated from Norris Junior High and entered North Bakersfield High School. I began a weekly discipleship meeting with our high school youth leader, which helped me grow in my faith like never before, and I emerged as a student leader in the campus ministry, <u>Fellowship of Christian Athletes.</u>

It was also in 1975 that Diana Ross asked the musical question, "*Do you know where you're going to?*" Churches concerned about the perceived decline of Christianity in America are asking the same question today.

They are at the proverbial crossroads: they can go north, east, west, or south, but they cannot *stay where they are*. Many perceive that if they choose wisely, they can stem the tide and restore their church to vibrant faith. But if they choose poorly, they may actually make matters *worse*.

This part of *Jesus Cropped from the Picture* represents the shaping factors of SLIM as I understand them from my life as a believer since 1975. It also outlines three forms of SLIM as I see them in the contemporary American church.

<u>Three Forms of SLIM</u>
Independent of each other, David Wells and Robert Webber described the manifestation of three prevailing methods that I am

calling Traditional, Pragmatic, and Emerging (see Appendix 5, "The Splintering of Western Protestantism).

Each method was formed out of the best of intentions for the glory of God and has been instrumental in the salvation of millions worldwide. However, each method represents a variation of SLIM (Spectator, Linguistic, Individual, Mental), defined by the following categories:

⋄ Assumptions about **culture**
⋄ View of **nostalgia** (what it considers to be "the good old days")
⋄ What it is reacting against (the common **antagonist**)

Assumptions About Culture

Culture is a *pattern of behavior, often expressed in terms of preferences for food, language, clothes, and a sense of what is beautiful or repulsive*. Culture is also defined by the rules that make sense of the world (its worldview).

Cultural differences are critical to the purposes of God. He shows his love of cultural diversity in the Abrahamic covenant to include "all peoples" in his redemption (Gen. 12.1-3), fulfilled at the consummation that includes "every tribe and language and people and nation" (Rev. 5.9). In fact, Jesus affirmed that the event which *triggers* his Second Coming is when the gospel of the Kingdom goes out as "a testimony to all nations" (Matt. 24.14).

When it comes to cultural differences, no other world religion is as hospitable as Christianity. Islam, Judaism, Hinduism, and other religions associate certain food, clothing, and activities as essential elements of their religious practices. However, in Christ, there is no "Christian"

106

food, clothing, or other cultural expression. God has made it possible for entire cultures to express their faith in Christ by *retaining* their cultural identity, not *losing* it. For example, Asian Christians will practice their faith in Christ differently than Africans, and Europeans different from Latinos.

As a result, the primary task of a missionary is to root through the elements of culture and separate them into three categories: those which are *consistent* with God's character (virtue); those which are *contrary* to God's character (vice or sin); and those which are *neutral* to God's character (neither virtue nor vice). Every culture has elements that are consistent with, contrary to, or neutral to God's character.

Contextualization

Another missionary task is called *contextualization*, the process of learning cultural elements of a people group so they can be employed to communicate the gospel. The goal is to eliminate *barriers* that hinder understanding, while creating *bridges to* the gospel message, so the receiving culture can hear the message, forming Christian expression within their indigenous culture.

But the process of contextualization is complicated. Two errors are possible. One is to be *too casual* regarding the receiving culture, forming an unhealthy blend of Christian faith and local culture. This is called "syncretism," where the "stamp of approval" of orthodox faith is given to a particular culture. An example was the blending of Latin American pagan rituals with Christian practices. Syncretism places too much in the "neutral" or "virtue" categories, and is not rigorous enough in its critique to place items in the "vice" category.

The opposite error of syncretism is "ethnocentrism," which assumes the sending missionary's culture is superior to the receiving culture. An example is the historic blunder of colonial missionaries who forced African people to wear western clothing. Ethnocentrism is *too aggressive in its critique* and inadvertently puts too much in the "vice" category instead of the "neutral" category.

The task of each church leader is to do what missionaries have done for years: sort through what is "virtue," what is "vice," and what is "neutral." Elders, pastors, bishops, and other leaders must know historic, orthodox, apostolic, biblical Christian faith so well that they can contextualize within their own culture without ethnocentricism or syncretism. But there are three challenges church leaders face as they do this task.

Lack of Historical Context
The biggest challenge to contextualization is that many church leaders have an inadequate grasp of historic, apostolic, Christian faith articulated by the Great Tradition (see Part Three).

Americans are generally disinterested in history and many church leaders lack an appreciation for Church history. Some may have known at one time, but have forgotten amidst all the clamor of cultural change and the madcap scramble to stay relevant. Others never really understood what historic faith meant. Finally, there are those *who think they know*, but do not. Without a proper understanding of historic Christian faith, contextualization is perilous.

Rapid Changes in American Culture

The second problem with contextualization in America is that there are so many sub-cultures emerging, and with such rapidity, that the cultural landscape is hard to describe. Many communities, and the churches within them, may be comprised of a number of competing sub-cultures, making it challenging to define. Los Angeles, the city where I minister, is arguably the most cosmopolitan city in the history of the planet.[70] Many other cities are becoming more diverse as well.

There are Postmoderns and Moderns, boomers and X-er's, first-generation immigrants from Asia, Central America, Africa, and Eastern Europe, not to mention partially acculturated groups like African-Americans, some of whom want to retain their historic identity, and others who want to assimilate into the dominant culture. The landscape is *so* dynamic, it is unclear what the America's dominant culture *is* anymore.

All of this cultural confusion makes it onerous to sort the cultural elements into neat cultural categories of *virtue, vice, and neutral,* making it more likely that church leaders will simply muddle along from day to day, hoping it will miraculously get better.

The Unseen Nature of Culture

The third obstacle in contextualization is that those living within a culture are the least likely to notice it. For example, it is easier for Americans to observe and describe European culture because they notice European deviations from American norms. Europeans, who are simply acting naturally, go about their daily routine without making reference to their own cultural assumptions. In the same way, Anglos are least likely to see their cultural preferences, whereas Hispanics and African Americans can point them out quite easily. Culture is like the air; the people within a culture cannot see it, nor are they aware of its existence from moment to moment.

This is why it can be difficult to identify the cultural elements of *Individualism* and *Rationalism* found in SLIM. These cultural assumptions are buried deep in the American psyche, especially in the church, where they have been erroneously placed in the *virtue* category of culture, instead of the *neutral* category where they belong. **SLIM has arguably slipped into the category of syncretism.**

<u>View of Nostalgia</u>
Besides culture, the three methods were formed by their favorite historical era. Each method has an unspoken sense of nostalgia about "the good old days." There is a deep desire to regain the "glory years," imagining a future that looks something like a bygone era. Some view the Reformation as the "Golden Era," and others idealize the early Church.

For others, the nostalgic era is a period of American history (such as the 1950s), or a time when their local church or denomination was at its peak. They reminisce about the days of old, when their church was growing in numbers, finances were not a problem, the music was good, and the preaching sound.

Common Antagonist

Besides its cultural assumptions and its sense of nostalgia, each of the three methods has a group or philosophy against which it is reacting. Each method is a corrective reaction to something that was not working at the time, or was no longer orthodox, like the Reformation's response to Roman Catholic abuses, conservatives' reaction to liberalism, or evangelicals' separation from fundamentalism.

Cultural assumptions, nostalgic eras, and *common antagonists* are the shaping forces that define the Traditional, Pragmatic, and Emerging methods, each of which promises to restore vibrant faith in America.

Chapter 13: The Traditional Method

ALL THREE OF the methods have a unique history. The Traditional Method can be traced to the splintering of Protestantism in the 1800s (see Appendix 5, "The Splintering of Western Protestantism"). Liberal Protestants, who desired to see Christian faith accepted among the intellectual elite, gave up Reformation beliefs about the authority and veracity of Scripture (*cropping Jesus out of the picture* in their own way). Those who stayed faithful to Reformation views of Scripture and other historical tenets of faith were called "conservatives." By the early part of the 20th century, liberals and conservatives had mostly separated from each other.

However, among conservative Protestants, debate continued over how long the list of essential elements of Christian faith should be. During the first half of the 20th century, "fundamentalists" suggested the list should be long, even if it meant excluding others or isolating themselves from the rest of the Church. Fundamentalists sought to prevent *Jesus from being cropped* by holding siege against attacks to their views of historic faith. "Evangelicals" believed the list of fundamentals should be short in order to reach as many people for Christ as possible.

By World War II, fundamentalists had retreated within themselves, devoting their energy to defending their view of orthodoxy. Evangelicals formed a consensus of various factions who became committed to two non-negotiable essentials: the *authority of Scripture* (The Bible) and an emphasis on Jesus' *substitutionary work of atonement through his death and resurrection* (The Cross). The Traditional Method was born out of this evangelical consensus. Adherents vigorously defended these two essentials because they represented the core principles of Christian faith. To live for Christ became equivalent to defense of this consensus (*the Bible and the Cross*).

The First Shaping Force: Cultural Assumptions

The Traditional Method's selection of *the Bible and the Cross* as its distinctives was partially influenced by the cultural assumptions of Rationalism and Individualism.

Rationalism

It can be argued that the focus on *The Cross* began around 1000 A.D., when the *Christus Victor* view of the atonement (all the saving acts of Christ) was supplanted by various one-dimensional views of the atonement. First, Anselm described Jesus' work on the cross, as a legal exchange for man's justification, based on the feudal culture of the day. *The Cross* began to take on a legal and rational quality. Later, other one-dimensional views of the atonement (such as Abelard's and Hodge's) emerged as well (see Appendix 5, "Views of the Atonement").

During the Reformation,[71] the Bible was emphasized as God's authoritative Word, supplanting the authority of the Roman Catholic Church. At the same time, the printing press allowed the wide distribution of the Bible to the masses. As Rationalism became widely accepted, the *individual Bible student* emerged for the first time. Later, the Age of Reason (or Modernity) made Rationalism the norm in Western culture, especially in the Protestant church.

By the 1800s, Rationalism became further entrenched after the splintering of Protestantism. As liberals attacked the Bible's authority, conservatives defended Scripture on the basis of reason, making Rationalism a primary way to express Christian faith. By the 1950s, the Traditional Method was birthed in the context of withering attacks on the Bible, coalescing around a Rationalistic defense of the Bible that could hold its ground against liberal skeptics.

Individualism through The Marketing Concept[72]

The gestation of the Traditional Method coincided with titanic shifts in American business practices. From the industrial revolution to the 1920s, the conventional wisdom in business was for a company to make products it could manufacture, offer those products at a low price, and then the demand for that product would take care of itself. This was called the "Production Concept." At that time, there were many customers, but not enough products to go around. Since consumers in the 1920s were eager for any low-priced product that met their basic needs, corporate sales forces and marketing techniques were rarely needed.

However, by the 1930s mass production had become common and there were more products available than there were people to buy them. In fact, consumer products were becoming so common that businesses had to increase advertising and hiring more sales personnel to convince consumers to buy their products. This was called the "Sales Concept." There was little attention paid to whether the consumer *needed* the product or not; the goal was to beat the competition, with little care for customer satisfaction.

After World War II, the amount of products and services exploded and the *Sales Concept* was no longer adequate. With a record amount of discretionary income, Americans could afford to be selective about the products they wanted. For the first time, they could choose among *multiple* products and began demanding specialized items to meet their wishes.

However, such wishes were not always transparent to companies, so they started asking: "What do customers want? Can we develop it while they still want it? How can we keep customers satisfied?" The entire organizational business enterprise suddenly shifted to *meet customer needs.*

The resulting shift was called the *Marketing Concept,* the belief that "the key to achieving organizational goals consists in determining the needs and wants of target markets and delivering the desired satisfactions more effectively and efficiently than competitors."[73] The *Marketing Concept* solidified the idea that "customer is king." Because of this titanic shift in business practice to the individual consumer, Individualism became embedded in American culture.

Rationalism and Individualism Mixed Together
In the 1950s, as Traditionals continued defending the Bible against liberal attacks, they were rapidly deploying missionaries and forming new publications, educational institutions, and parachurch organizations. It was an exciting time of growth.

Meanwhile, the *Marketing Concept* was developing in America without much notice from Traditionals. Without knowing it, the Traditional Method and the *Marketing Concept* were growing up together. Both were influencing American culture, resulting in a new mix of American Christianity, where biblical (Rational) truth was slowly being perceived as a "product" that would be good for the individual. As business language become more common in the culture, Christians began talking about their faith in business terms. For example, Americans' view of the Bible was gradually transforming into an authoritative *consumer owner's manual* to help the individual Christian.

As a result, American Christianity was morphing into an individualized and rational pursuit of Bible knowledge and personal ethics, made possible by Jesus' death on the cross *(for personal salvation).* Even the sacraments focused on the individual (rather than on Christ's victory over the powers of evil). Baptism was no longer a renunciation of loyalty from one kingdom to another Kingdom, but increasingly a public acknowledgment of Jesus' work for *personal salvation.* Communion's purposes narrowed to a remembrance of the cross *(for personal salvation).* The celebrations of Jesus' many past, present, and future triumphs on the Church's behalf was disappearing.

Therefore, many Traditionals believed they simply needed to grow in their knowledge of *the Bible* (Rationalism) and live a moral life in grateful response to Jesus' substitutionary work on *the cross* (Individualism). None of this was wrong, but it reduced the Christian faith in a way it had never been reduced before. Because of these cultural assumptions, one Traditional recently summarized his faith as adherence to "revealed truth, doctrine that is to be believed, moral norms that should be followed, and church life in which participation is expected."[74]

The Second Shaping Force: Nostalgic Era

The Traditional Method values one of five nostalgic eras (for more detailed discussion, see Appendix 5).

The Protestant Reformation

For most Traditionals, the Reformation was a day of renewal and clear teaching that articulated biblical orthodoxy for hundreds of years. The Reformation continues to offer the defining marks of the Church, where the Word of God is preached, the sacraments are rightly administered, and discipline is applied. For many, this is the ideal to which churches should return.

Happy Days

A second nostalgic era for Traditionals is the 1950s. It was a time of enthusiasm and creative energy. Evangelical publications were born, missionaries were commissioned like never before, Christian schools were opened and new ministries were formed, promising to affect the world for Christ. Influential leaders like Billy Graham, John Stott, and J.I. Packer emerged as leading voices during this time.

The 1950s was also a time of optimism in America, as the country became the world's leader in business, government, and the military. Many Traditionals long to go back to this period as a time when Traditional mores were accepted in society, prior to the decline of morality in the 1960s.

The Early Church

Another possible nostalgic era for Traditionals is the early church, as described in the New Testament. Through misapplication of "sola scriptura," and suspicion of the Roman Catholic Church, some Traditionals make a wholesale dismissal of the lessons of Church history. For them, Scripture is the *only* source of ecclesiology, viewing New Testament practices as prescriptive for contemporary church settings.

The Glory Days

Some Traditionals long for a specific period when *their local church* was at its height. For example, a church may recall the 1970s (or 1980s) when programs were vital, attendance was high, and the future looked bright. After this period, the church may have maintained its vitality, but never as much as "the glory days." For this kind of Traditional, this "gold standard" era is used to measure all current church activities.

Frontier Revivalism

The final sentimental era is *Frontier Revivalism*, an American phenomenon of the Great Awakenings of 1730-1840, where traveling evangelists preached compelling sermons to large crowds in frontier towns, inviting them to turn to Christ for salvation. For some Traditionals, especially those who frequently mention the need for revival, this was an idyllic time that needs to be recovered.

Frontier Revivalists changed the goal of preaching.[75] Historically, the Church had taught that every member should function within a local church that represents Jesus Christ against the principalities and powers of evil. The Revivalists shifted this perspective from a *corporate proclamation* of the Lordship of Jesus, to an attempt to make *individual converts*.

Jesus Cropped from the Picture

The theology of Revivalism did not discuss God's Kingdom purpose and put little emphasis on the Church. The goal was to bring *individual* sinners to an *individual* decision, for an *individualistic* faith. John Wesley understood the dangers of Frontier Revivalism when he said, "Christianity is essentially a social religion…to turn it into solitary religion is indeed to destroy it."[76]

An example of Revivalist assumptions was D.L. Moody's influential 19th century ministry. His message centered on salvation for the individual sinner, encapsulated in the Three R's: Ruined by sin, Redeemed by Christ, and Regenerated by the Spirit. Moody's gospel presentation, however, left out the larger Kingdom purpose of God that goes far beyond personal salvation. His teaching furthered a one-dimensional view of the atonement.

For Moody, the church was a voluntary association of saved individuals. His influence was so great that by the 1870s the Church was no longer seen as a grand corporate body, but as a *gathering of individuals.*[77] This emphasis has persisted as part of the bones and marrow of the Traditional Method today.

Frontier Revivalism also shifted the focus from the *message* to the *messenger.* More emphasis was placed on *how well someone could deliver a message.* Over time, it became assumed that the *number* of conversions was directly related to the speaker's *ability* to communicate. This idea unintentionally transformed the American preacher into a celebrity.

A final effect of Frontier Revivalism is its contribution to America's fascination with their *inner life.* Before Revivalism, self-love was viewed as the root of original sin, but revivalists used it as motivation for conversion. Michael Horton contended, "Liberals and revivalists both de-emphasize God's transcendence and tend to see God's Word as something that wells up within a person rather than as something that comes to a person from the outside."[78] In some ways, the American fixation with introspection can be traced to Frontier Revivalism.

The Third Shaping Force: Common Antagonist

The Traditional Method has three primary antagonists. One is the Roman Catholic Church, against whom the Protestant Reformers reacted. Many Traditionals continue to have a negative view of Roman Catholicism. In fact, some Traditionals speak as though the Reformation were still in process today.

This general suspicion of the Roman Catholic Church extends to the devotional writings of non-Protestants throughout the ages, leaving Traditionals without the treasured wisdom of Aquinas, John of the Cross, Julian of Norwich, and Teresa of Avila.

The second antagonist is liberal Christianity, or its non-Christian counterpart, secular humanism. Since the Traditional Method was born out of conflict with liberal views of Scripture, it is easy to understand why liberalism is an antagonist. Even today, conflicts continue over the trustworthiness of the Bible, and much energy is directed to developing answers to skeptics' questions.

In recent years, the Emerging Method (with its embrace of Post-modernity) has become a bewildering antagonist to some Traditionals. Although Emergings come from a Traditional background, they are more open to Roman Catholicism and liberalism, which can be perplexing to a Traditional mind. As a result, Traditionals often find Emergings (and Postmodernity) difficult to categorize, and sometimes count them as a threat.

Focus of Energy

The Traditional Method is defined by its loyalty to a *Rationalistic Bible* and the *Cross (for personal salvation)*, longs for the glory days (The Reformation, the 1950s, or some other period), and is allied against the Roman Catholic Church, liberalism, or Postmodernity. Because of these factors, the Traditional Method focuses its energy on a return to a Rationalistic emphasis on the Bible as a means of combating its antagonists. Therefore, their slogan could be:

"Give me that old time religion, it's good enough for me."

Chapter 14: The Pragmatic Method

THE PRAGMATIC METHOD grew out of the churches and ministries formed by the Traditional Method from the 1950s to the 1970s.[79] With the *Marketing Concept* left mostly unchallenged, Traditionals grew up accepting Individualism as a normal way of life. By the 1970s, new marketing techniques encouraged committed Christians to format the gospel into messages that were easy to communicate and mass produce. Thus, the Pragmatic Method was an *attempt to use contemporary marketing concepts to preach the gospel to all nations.*

Also, the social upheaval of the 1960s left the Traditional Method shaken. The old ways were being questioned and Pragmatics recognized that churches needed to react to the cultural shifts. They understood the local church was no longer the only place to "be fed." Christians could get teaching from radio, television, and other recorded media.

Further, non-Christians had more leisure opportunities than ever before, and suddenly local churches found themselves vying for attention with society's alternatives. Churches also realized they were in competition with one another for a shrinking number of church-goers. In order to survive, churches and denominations felt pressure to find ways to reach a wider audience, communicate more effectively, and package the gospel message in its simplest form.

In general, Pragmatics are those who came to faith between 1975 and 2000 and were influenced by the changes in the American church during this period (see Appendix 5, "The Splintering of Western Protestantism").

Undermining The Local Church

During the 1950s, as the Traditional Method was forming, parachurch institutions were created to strengthen the Church. But by the 1970s and 1980s, the same organizations that had once supported local churches began to unintentionally *undermine* the local church.

For example, student-led campus ministries joined in the attempt to simplify the gospel for mass appeal, especially to intellectual college students. During the early 1980s, I was as a leader of two such groups, Fellowship of Christian Athletes, and InterVarsity Christian Fellowship. My co-laborers and I pursued new ways to share the gospel and disciple new believers. Our goal was to bring as many as possible to personal faith in Christ, as quickly as possible.

Since we did not fully understand the biblical teaching that the Church was Jesus' agent of the Kingdom, we offered faith *separated from* Church and made local church attendance *optional*. Many of us taught that the campus ministry could be the believer's source of individual feeding and fellowship. Therefore, believers were free to attend a local church if it met their needs and schedule, but as long as they were being fed and growing in Christ, they did not need a local church to live a Christian life.

Because we viewed churches as alternative "feeding" providers, it was not an exaggeration to say that we thought the *First Presbyterian Church* was to Burger King as *InterVarsity* was to McDonalds. By the

1980s, Pragmatics like me began to think of themselves as *Christians apart from the local church*. Christianity had become a personal relationship between "me and God."

Those who *did* attend church began to choose a church that fit their personal preferences, much like a people would shop for a family car. In response, churches began to design their programs and activities to draw in members based on their stated needs, which often coincided with contemporary tastes in American entertainment. The Pragmatic Method embraced a faith that was individualistic, self-focused, and consumer-oriented. Instead of seeing this as a weakness to be resisted, Pragmatics used it as an opportunity to be exploited. Entrepreneurial success replaced faithfulness to the *Story of the Kingdom*.

A Shift in Emphasis

The Pragmatic Method continued the Traditional's commitments to a *Rationalistic Bible* and the *Cross (for personal salvation)* as basic tenets of orthodoxy, but the efforts shifted to *optimum communication* of the Bible and the Cross, as evidenced *in the numbers*. The new questions were, "Are we filling the pews? Is the message persuasive and attractive? How many people are responding? Are we meeting people's felt-needs?"

These Pragmatic assumptions can be recognized by the way a church attracts new attenders. For example, a Pragmatic church might describe itself as "a friendly and warm church with active programs and a vital worship experience that is second to none. We have a fun youth ministry where it is safe to bring your children." The emphasis is on programs and activities that attract people to have their personal needs met. An example can be seen in Figure 15.[80]

Hi Neighbor!

At last! A new church for those who have given up on church services! Let's face it. Many people aren't active in church these days.
WHY?

Too often
– the sermons are boring and don't relate to daily living
– many churches seem more interested in your wallet than in you
– members are unfriendly to visitors
– you wonder about the quality of the nursery care for your little ones

Do you think attending church should be enjoyable? WELL, WE'VE GOT GOOD NEWS FOR YOU!

Valley Church is a new church designed to meet your needs in the 1990's. At Valley Church you
– Meet new friends and get to know your neighbors
– Enjoy exciting music with a contemporary flavor
– Hear a positive, practical message which uplifts you each week
    - How to feel good about yourself
    - How to overcome depression
    - How to have a full and successful life
    - Learning to handle your money without it handling you
    - The secrets of successful family living
    - How to overcome stress
– Trust your children to the care of dedicated nursery workers

WHY NOT GET A LIFT INSTEAD OF A LETDOWN THIS SUNDAY?

Figure 15: A Pragmatic Church Advertisement

Another way to recognize a Pragmatic mindset is by their emphasis on numbers as evidence of spiritual fruit. For example, my wife and I are members of an adult Sunday school class called "Epic," which was formed to help us shift perspective from "worship as seminar" to "worship as celebration" (see Chapter 6). When the class started, what most friends wanted to know was *how many people* were in attendance, as though numbers were an indication of success. Their queries indicated the influence of the Pragmatic Method.

Cultural Assumptions

The Pragmatic Method was heavily influenced by the *Marketing Concept*. While the Traditional Method silently accepted it as a "neutral" cultural expression, Pragmatics co-opted it as a "virtue," making it the central mechanism for church outreach in the mid-1970s. Since the *Marketing Concept* always starts with *the customer*, churches began orienting their programs and activities around the needs of the unchurched individual.

The Pragmatic Method seeks to design programs that harness God's power in order to produce predictable results.[81] For example, many churches joined in the 1976 *I Found It* campaign, a mass-communication effort using the latest marketing principles to share the gospel. As a young Christian participating in the campaign, I was taught to make telemarketing calls to share the gospel and respond to consumer questions. The program was geared toward personal salvation (Individualism), provided answers to skeptics' queries (Rationalism), and made church membership optional (although church participation was highly encouraged).

The Bible

Pragmatics believe that the Bible is not only true, but also *good for the individual*, providing not only the message of eternal life in the age to come, but help for life on earth as well. With the Bible as the "owner's manual," church leaders aggressively applied marketing principles to draw people to Christian faith. The assumption was that anyone presented with the right message would naturally "buy into" personal faith in Christ.

In the mid-1980s, I earned my MBA, taking a number of graduate marketing classes, including one class called "Consumer Decision Behavior." Consumerism had become a science that was quickly penetrating mainstream American culture, and the Pragmatic church as well. Since then, marketing language has become commonplace in the church, such as "finding a niche for our church." By 1988, Barna went so far to say, "My contention, based on careful study of data and the activities of American churches, is that the major problem plaguing the church is its failure to embrace a marketing orientation in what has become a market-driven environment."[82]

As the *Marketing Concept* became acceptable, the new sovereign king was the *individual consumer*. In a subtle way Jesus was no longer King of his Kingdom. Jesus was *cropped from the picture*.

Lost Discipleship
Pragmatics believed the gospel message needed to be concise and attractive. The new paradigm was that once people made a "purchase decision" (accepting Christ as savior), they could be grounded in the more complicated or unpleasant aspects of discipleship at a later time. It made no sense to introduce potential believers to all the complexities of Christianity when it was as simple as "accepting Christ's payment of sin on the cross."

Since churches designed their services and activities to draw in outsiders, they attempted to "keep everything simple and light." But in this environment, once a person received Christ, there were few opportunities to hear about the deeper and more challenging aspects of discipleship. As new believers became older believers, they were ill-equipped to disciple new converts because they, themselves, had never been oriented to the fullness of following Christ.

The New High Priests

The 1970s also brought a new openness to the self-actualization movement that started in the 1960s. With it came a fresh interest in introspection and psychological health. This found its way into the church as a method for securing a good life, where the Bible was viewed as the *ultimate resource* for mental health.

So while Traditionals had revered the pastor as the "man in the pulpit" (the primary source of biblical truth), Pragmatics began to view the pastor as the first stop for personal counseling. If the pastor could not provide helpful advice, then professional counseling was available as a fallback solution. With the advancement of psychology as a legitimate science, many Christians believed that therapists had the most effective (Rationalistic) means of dealing with the difficulties of life (Individualism). As a result, counselors surpassed pastors as the new "high priests" of their Pragmatic faith.

Celebrity Pastors

The Traditionals' view of the pastor was someone who was "as comfortable with books and learning as with the aches of the soul, who each Sunday took the flock into the treasures of God's Word."[83]

Jesus Cropped from the Picture

The Pragmatic Method altered these expectations. The pastor went from being a *trusted shepherd* to a *celebrity communicator*.

Frontier Revivalism (see Chapter 13) had propagated the idea that effective communication was necessary to yield the most converts, and by the 1970s, five decades of Hollywood's star-making industry had made the celebrity a central fixture of American life. The proliferation of television and other media advertising, along with the *Marketing Concept*, made it natural to assume that a church needed an attractive, articulate, and charismatic leader if their church was going to be healthy (as measured by attendance).

A few years ago, I witnessed the manifestation of this misguided thinking during a congregational meeting to consider a pastoral candidate. One man asked for the microphone and quoted Barna's research on the need to have a *world-class communicator*. Apparently having no need to spare the feelings of the highly-qualified candidate standing in front of the congregation, the man proceeded to lament why a more charismatic speaker could not be found. He said, "After all, we live in Burbank, the media capital of the world. Couldn't we find someone better to speak to this culture?" As many people nodded their heads in agreement, his ridiculous assumptions went unchallenged.

Nostalgic Era

Because the Pragmatic Method values "what works for me," it is difficult to define a specific nostalgic era. History holds little interest to Pragmatics unless it has some direct relevance to their personal lives, so very few will make reference to the Reformation or other periods of church history. Pragmatics do not have a common set of doctrines but are held together by their desire to *meet the needs of the individual.* Therefore, each Pragmatic might have a different idea about what the "glory years" were.

For most, it was the age that was most personally satisfying to them as an *individual.* For example, many Boomers view the 1960s as the best days of their lives, while others see the 1970s or 1980s as idyllic. Some people look back to a time when they received Christ, or a time when they were vibrant in their personal faith; a season of life when they were growing in the Lord. They often engage in a life-long pursuit to "get that feeling again."

Common Antagonist

The Pragmatic Method is against whatever "does not work." So Pragmatics react against the Traditional Method for being too "churchy," which, they believe, drives people away from the church. Each Pragmatic church sees itself in the process of survival; in competition with other churches or with activities that keep people away from church services.

David Wells expressed the fears of Pragmatics this way:

[They are] pushed along by the sense that things are stagnating in the evangelical world and the ways of "doing" church in the past won't work with newer generations. That being so, churches must change their way of doing business or face extinction … Church is like a product now being rendered obsolete by the passage of time and the onrush of innovation.[84]

Because of this need for survival, Pragmatics may embrace some of the techniques of the Emerging Method (Chapter 15), but only when it works at *drawing people in*. They will not ally with the Emerging Method on matters of principle, but they will on pragmatic grounds.

Sometimes Pragmatics despise their own assumptions but do not know how to be released from them. Hugh Halter said:

> We show up at church to get what we want (which is feeding from a leader), not what we need (to feed ourselves and others). And if we don't get what we want we head to the basilica next door because that chaplain is better at giving us what we want. Although frustrated by the consumer approach of their adherents, the modern-day paid pastors don't feel they can lead the way their hearts tell them to for fear of losing a tithing attender. Often, the pressure is so strong, they find themselves frantically trying to update their presentation, increase programs to attract people, or lighten up the message of the gospel. Basically we're just playing musical pews.[85]

Focus of Energy

The Pragmatic Method focuses its energy on constantly shifting to meet consumer demand in order to maintain attendance and support the budget. Pragmatic churches incorporate media and theatrical approaches to reach the unchurched. Pastors feel the pressure to eliminate parts of church life that are unpleasant. Since Pragmatics are fearful about becoming obsolete and irrelevant, they tend to hire staff who specialize in making church life "fun." Because of the need to respond to market changes, there is a myriad of "how-to" techniques, implying the extinction of the Church unless the proper expertise is skillfully applied.

A prominent example is Willlow Creek Church's 2007 market research study, called **Reveal**. Willow Creek, a prototype of the Pragmatic Method, publically announced that something was wrong in their approach to church. A customer survey reported that those who were *most centered on Jesus were the most disappointed with church and most likely to leave*. However, those who were new to their faith found church the most satisfying. Willow Creek concluded that their programs were good at attracting new people to faith, but ineffective in preventing boredom for veterans.

Willow Creek's leaders said, "Some of the stuff that we have put millions of dollars into thinking it would really help our people grow and develop spiritually, when the data actually came back it wasn't helping people that much.... We made a mistake.... Our dream is that we fundamentally change the way we do church. That we take out a clean sheet of paper and we rethink all of our old assumptions. Replace it with new insights. Insights that are informed by research and rooted in Scripture."[86]

Notice the Pragmatic cultural influences underlying Reveal. They started with the customer (Individualism) and then conducted a survey (Rationalism) to determine how the customer felt (Individualism), relative to the services offered (*Marketing Concept*). They placed a high value on research and analysis (more Rationalism). The nature of their customer survey put highest value on the individual relationship with Christ (Individualism). Not surprisingly, the longer believers were nurtured in this SLIM environment, the more disaffected they became, and the more likely they were to leave the church. Those who were new to a SLIM approach found it new and exciting at first, but it wore thin over time.

Rather than cease their SLIM approaches and chart an EPIC course, they considered how to make their activities even *more targeted to the individual.* For example, one of their options was to provide believers with a spiritual mentor, akin to a personal trainer,[87] to help individuals experience their own personal spiritual fulfillment and growth (more Individualism), rather than re-orient believers to contribution to the Kingdom.

Instead of catering to a personal desire to be "spiritually fit,"a better approach would be to orient new believers to their Kingdom identity, as *People of the Story.*

The Pragmatic Method is formed by the *Marketing Concept*, defines nostalgia in a personal way, and fights against anything that competes with church attendance. For the Pragmatic, the current church decline is especially distressing because the pressure is on to find a clever marketing solution. Because of these factors, their slogan could be:

"Does it work? If not, we need to fix it."

Chapter 15: The Emerging Method

THE EMERGING METHOD has its roots in the Traditional and Pragmatic methods. It shares many of their commitments to the Bible, Christ's redemptive work, and making the gospel understandable to the culture.

However, it seeks to break away from the Traditional and Pragmatic methods over their use of Rationalism (or "Modernity"). The Emerging Method appeared in the 1990s in an attempt to contextualize the gospel in a Postmodern culture. Many of its members are young people who have come to faith in Christ since 2000 (see Appendix 5, "The Splintering of Western Protestantism"). Despite these general parameters, finding a precise definition of the Emerging Method is a formidable task.

First, the Emerging Method runs along a spectrum from those who are *closely committed to historic Christian faith* to those who have *abandoned the authority of Scripture* and are more like liberals than conservatives. Within the same Emerging church there can be a variety of commitments to apostolic, orthodox faith.

Second, Emergings resist characterizing themselves in precise terms. They are suspicious of propositional statements stated in categorical terms,[88] especially with respect to theology (for example, "The truth about God is ___"). They are pessimistic about the shelf-life of what others view as "transcendent, objective truth." Third, any movement is difficult to define during its infancy, especially one using "emerging" as its moniker.

Jesus Cropped from the Picture

Cultural Assumptions

Postmodern culture is the driving force of the Emerging Method. While Traditionals and Pragmatics are less aware that they were formed by cultural factors, Emergings embrace the influence culture plays on how people understand their faith. In fact, in many respects, the Emerging Method *originates from the place of culture.*[89]

Emergings appear confident that their *pessimism toward transcendent truth* will be the last and most complete phase of human philosophy, and that nothing superior can supplant it. Therefore, they look forward to a continuing emergence in which their philosophy engulfs the outdated notions of the Traditional and Pragmatic methods. Theirs is a new, exciting pursuit of truth, experienced through their personal and corporate faith journeys.

Rationalism and the Bible

Placing limited value on Rationalism, Emergings react against the Traditionals' commitments to the Bible in *strictly rational ways*. They do not react against the Bible as much as they dislike the *rational approaches* Traditionals employ. Emergings prefer to engage theology as a *conversation*. They recognize the Bible as an authoritative source of God's narrative, but do not value Scripture in the Linguistic-Mental way the Traditional Method does.

In contrast to the Pragmatic and Traditional methods, who emphasize the *accumulation of information* as the measure of maturity, Emergings are more interested in *personal transformation*. Emergings seek *authentic discipleship and genuine experience* over the Pragmatic's self-help and "information transfer."[90]

However, like the Pragmatic and Traditional methods, Emergings have a "pick and choose" approach to the Scriptures based on what seems most relevant to the individual. The individual is sovereign, not the biblical Story that has been believed for centuries. As Emerging Church author Scot McKnight said, "We believe the Great Tradition offers various ways for telling the truth about God's redemption in Christ, but we don't believe any one theology gets it absolutely right."[91] David Wells observes that for Emergings, "Christianity is about filling out *my* story, being propelled on *my* journey by the Scriptures or the Holy Spirit, and being propelled into the (post)modern world. It is not about our fitting into the *Bible's* narrative."[92] Such individualistic notions *crop Jesus from the picture*.

Emergings prefer to talk about "narratives" rather than systematic theology, so they are often suspicious of a single, authoritative *meta-narrative* (a narrative that explains everything). At best, Emergings are humble about their ability to know truth in an objective way.[93] At worst, Emergings lack submission to Christ's command to believe the entire scriptural narrative[94] (the scriptures that testify about Jesus, John 5.39).

Contextualizing

Emergings seem to assume they already understand the gospel and are equipped to contextualize it in a Postmodern setting. However, this is not a good assumption. Many Emergings come from Traditional or Pragmatic backgrounds and bring some of their *cropped-out-of-the-picture* assumptions with them. In their worthy attempt to challenge the Church to more serious discipleship, Emerging Christians rush past the need to have an objective definition of Christian faith.

In too many cases, the *individual* Emerging, not the *Story of God's work throughout history,* becomes the arbiter of truth. As Gibbs and Bolger said, "In a time of immense cultural change and disconnect with the church, emerging churches retrieved the Jesus of the Gospels, but not necessarily the Christ of history."[95] Therefore, their incoherent identity leaves them without sufficient traction to contextualize. A better approach would be to start with a definitive understanding of the Kingdom Story, *then* contextualize in the culture of Postmodernity.

Community

Emergings react against the privatized faith of Traditionals and Pragmatics, preferring to self-actualize in small, connected groups.[96] They seek to distance themselves from a focus on personal relevance by living their faith in community. But the reality is they search for *personal* truth within a community of faith, where worshipers pursue an experience with God through a variety of individualistic ways. The *individual* is the one who determines what is acceptable worship. As one Emerging said, "Begin to express yourself using tools that you understand. You may understand graphic design; you may understand Bulgarian nose flutes; the media is irrelevant."[97]

While they value community, they continue the Pragmatic's view that institutions are required to serve the *individual*.[98] Some Emergings require gatherings to be relevant to a much greater degree than Pragmatics. "We want creativity, artistic expression, and to hear from one another. A meeting is only as good as the purpose behind it."[99]

Instead of starting with an objective, historic, and creedal understanding of Christian faith, Emergings seek to discover the meaning of their personal lives as they intersect their subjective, emerging version of the gospel. In these cases, where the importance of subjective, personal experience is elevated above historic faith, *Emergings are Pragmatics on steroids.*

Most Emergings would be critical of SLIM (Spectator, Linguistic, Individual, Mental). In this respect, the Emerging Method is serving as a healthy improvement to SLIM Christian faith. However, while they may describe themselves as EPIC (Experiential, Participative, Image-rich, Christ-centered), they are so highly *individualistic* in their approaches that their method is yet another variation of SLIM. Despite all the good they are doing, the Emerging Method still *crops Jesus from the picture.*

Nostalgic Era

Many in the Emerging Method desire to return to the early church prior to Constantine (see Appendix 5). Contemporary writers refer to Constantine as though he ended the Church age and ushered in an institutional church (Christendom), from which Christianity has never recovered. Their hope is that the Emerging Method will restore authentic Christian faith.[100]

They search intently for ways to re-employ early-church commitments to Jesus' teaching, community living, and the re-integration of the sacred and secular (see Chapter 7).[101] The Emerging Method is open to incorporating ancient practices into their worship, as long as they are not part of Christendom.

Common Antagonist

Emergings often react to the hypocrisy and shallowness they see in the Traditional and Pragmatic methods. This is why some Emergings call themselves "postevangelicals."[102] They desire a faith that is authentic, relevant, and permeates their actions. They crave "deeds, not creeds," and are antagonistic to Rationalistic or commercialized expressions of faith.[103]

Personal Salvation versus Missional Ethics
In an effort to separate from the shallowness of privatized faith, some Emergings believe that emphasis on "personal salvation" can be a distraction that should be avoided. Instead, Emergings attempt to shift the attention from Jesus' *work on the cross* to Jesus' *teachings and example*, especially the Sermon on the Mount.[104]

They believe the life and teachings of Jesus (which they call being "missional") offer a fresher and more authentic set of ethics. This missional approach is so paramount that they sometimes speak as though "the Kingdom" is synonymous with "missional." In some respects, the Emergings' passion for *missional ethics* has replaced the Traditionals' priority for *personal holiness.*

The Emergings' focus on being missional is admirable, but can inadvertently *crop Jesus from the picture* by minimizing the cross and the other works of Christ. *Christ's missional teachings* can become the new "one-dimensional approach" to Christianity. Michael Horton said, "When the focus of mission and ministry is on our *kingdom living* rather than on the one who brought and brings his own kingdom, ushering us and our hearers into it through his gospel, Christ-as-example can just as effectively replace Christ-as-Savior at least in practice."[105]

Politics

Emergings are uncomfortable with the perceived connection between the Traditional Method and conservative politics, seeing parallels with Constantine's Christendom and recent American civic religion. As a result they tend to be less conservative in their politics than Traditionals.

Focus of Energy

The Emerging Method seeks to contextualize Christianity within Postmodern culture. In an effort to live out their missional under-standing of the gospel, Emergings are eager to "welcome the stranger, serve with generosity, participate as producers, create as created beings, lead as a body, and take part in spiritual activities."[106] They emphasize service to the poor as a way of life (not just as a program) and use their vocations as a means of fleshing out the gospel, emphasizing the church *dispersed*[107] more than the church *gathered* (see Chapter 8). Finally, Emergings seek to make theology less divisive by encouraging open dialogue and resisting a "thick line" that separates insiders from outsiders.

Because Emergings are experimenting with Postmodern ways to live the life of Jesus in community, their slogan could be:

"Is it authentic and relevant?"

Chapter 16: How Jesus Was Cropped from the Picture

THE TRADITIONAL, PRAGMATIC, and Emerging methods are three distinct expressions of SLIM, each of which has *cropped Jesus from the picture*. Figure 16 summarizes the approaches and assumptions of each method:

Traditional	Pragmatic	Emerging
Starting Point		
Reaction to liberalism	Individual consumer	Postmodern culture
Cultural assumptions		
Rationalism, one-dimensional (cross-centered) view of atonement	Marketing Concept, therapeutic approaches	Postmodernity, personal relevance
Foundational principle		
Reformation	My personal relationship	Jesus' teaching and example (missional)
Communication emphasis		
Rationalistic Bible; Personal salvation (Cross)	Reduction of message for mass appeal	My narrative meets God's narrative
Era of nostalgia		
1950s	A personally meaningful decade or season of life	Pre-Constantine
Common antagonist		
Liberalism, Roman Catholicism	Competing forces for church attendance	Modernity, Christendom

Figure 16: The Three Methods

Traditional	Pragmatic	Emerging
Biblical lens		
Rational	Pragmatic	Narrative
Subject		
The Rescue	Individual	Individual
Object		
Christ	Christ	Christ
Focus of energy		
Go back to glory days	Find what works	Be missional in Postmodernity
Slogan		
Be biblical	Be effective	Be relevant

Figure 16, continued: The Three Methods

During the first 1000 years of the Church, Jesus (Christus Victor) and his Story of the advancing Kingdom was the predominant view. The cultural and philosophical forces that ensued over the last centuries have slowly *cropped Jesus from the picture* of his own Story, reducing what was once an epic, awe-inspiring, ominous, and larger-than-life view of the world to the point that Christus Victor can hardly be recognized in the American church.

Before it was miniaturized, the Story included:

◇ Multiple aspects of Christ's saving work
◇ Narrative <u>and</u> rational components
◇ Christ as **SUBJECT** and the Church as **OBJECT**
◇ The <u>whole</u> Bible as God's Story
◇ Transcendent scope and depth

144

After the work of Anselm and Abelard (see Appendix 5, Views of the Atonement), the church lost the multiple dimensions of the atonement (Christus Victor) and the devil was partially cropped from the picture. Webber said, "The missing link in Western theology is a deep appreciation for the incarnation and subsequent Christus Victor theme of how God incarnate won a victory over sin and death."[108]

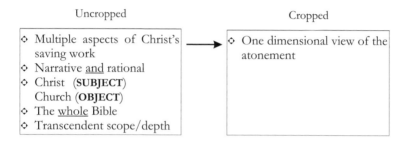

At the Reformation, a Rationalistic and Individualistic view of the Bible emerged, cropping the Bible's narrative quality:

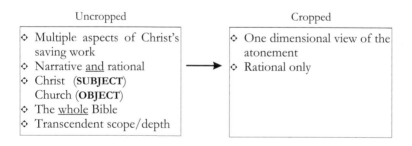

Jesus Cropped from the Picture

Frontier Revivalism and the *Marketing Concept* put the individual's salvation, inner life, and consumer needs at the forefront of faith, making the <u>Rescue</u> the new **SUBJECT**, relegating Christ as the **OBJECT**:

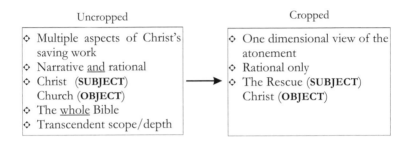

With the Traditional Method, the rich Story of Christ was reduced to *a Rationalistic Bible and the Cross (for personal salvation)*. With the Pragmatic Method, the Bible was abbreviated to become a consumer owner's manual, and Christianity was packaged in easy-to-understand messages that would attract non-believers to faith in Christ. The individual became the new **SUBJECT**, replacing "the <u>Rescue</u>,"and the Church became obsolete:

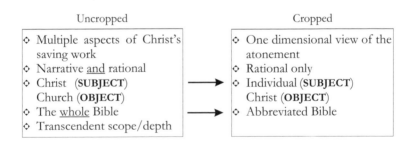

With Postmodernity, what was once a rich and transcendent view of Christ was distilled to appeal to a culture overloaded with information, inundated by quick and powerful images, handicapped by a short attention span, and abandoned to interpret the message through their subjective, individual experience:

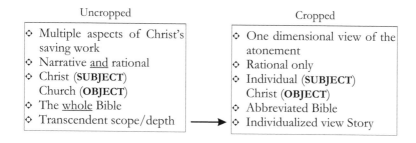

Uncropped	Cropped
◇ Multiple aspects of Christ's saving work	◇ One dimensional view of the atonement
◇ Narrative <u>and</u> rational	◇ Rational only
◇ Christ (**SUBJECT**) Church (**OBJECT**)	◇ Individual (**SUBJECT**) Christ (**OBJECT**)
◇ The <u>whole</u> Bible	◇ Abbreviated Bible
◇ Transcendent scope/depth	◇ Individualized view Story

What was once EPIC in nature had become hopelessly SLIM (see Figure 17). Christ was no longer the victorious King who triumphs over the devil through the Church, but an historical figure who died for "my personal salvation," and asks people to study his owner's manual in order to be ethical people until he returns to take them to heaven.

Figure 17: From Christ to Individual

147

Jesus Cropped from the Picture

Jesus has been *cropped from the picture.*

This cropping process spoiled the chances for Christians to enjoy all the riches of historic, orthodox faith by placing themselves in the center of the Story. It is no wonder American Christians are bored and longing for renewal.

....

Conclusion

My journey brought me to an important plateau. I had found the sources of decline represented in three contemporary methods: Traditional, Pragmatic, and Emerging, each of which is formed by the cultural forces that shaped it, the era it wants to return to, and the antagonists with which it contends.

The Traditional Method says, "Place more emphasis on a Rationalistic use of the Bible, through a personal-salvation focus of the atonement, in order to defeat our antagonists. Christians will be restored to vibrant faith if we go back to what worked in one of the nostalgic eras."

The Pragmatic Method says, "Make a better marketing appeal through programs, presentation, and activities for the sake of Christ. Come up with better ideas to draw people in."

The Emerging Method says, "Be more relevant to Postmodern culture for the sake of Christ. Go back to what the Church was before Constantine and restore the Church to what it should be."

Despite these artificially clean categories, navigating a church through these waters is not easy. For example, a church might have a Traditional pastor, an Emerging youth leader, and a Pragmatic chair of the elder board, none of whom can articulate their presuppositions, each confused by their friendly conflict, not knowing the reasons why.

Church leaders may be confused about what they believe and may go through phases: trying Pragmatic approaches, then upon failure, attempting Emerging principles, followed by a season of going back to Traditional practices.

The voices can be maddening: Be more biblical! Make sure it works! Be more relevant! Or there are many other distracting alternatives formed by culture, nostalgia, and common antagonists. How can church leaders find a way out of this mess? How can the picture be de-cropped to include Jesus, while allowing each church to retain its heritage, values, and traditions? These were the final questions I needed to answer before my journey was complete.

Part Three (Back to the Future) will explain the satisfying end of my search. I found rest when I discovered a way back to the full picture of Jesus and his Kingdom Story, where Christians could be restored to vibrant faith.

♯

Holy Spirit, guide us in the complexity of this age. There are so many competing voices shouting at us. We need your direction to point us back to the Lord Jesus Christ.

Part Three: Back to the Future

"Next Saturday night, we're sending you back
to the future!"

- Dr. Emmett Brown, <u>Back to the Future</u>

....

The Traditional, Emerging, and Pragmatic methods seek to revitalize vibrant faith, but end up cropping Jesus from the big picture of Scripture. The best way to restore Christians to vibrant theology, worship, discipleship, and outreach is to recapture the Church's identity as People of the Story, through a re-connection to the Church's Sacred Roots.

Chapter 17: The Satisfying End of My Journey

IN PART ONE, the source of "this provincial life" was expressed in terms of *SLIM*, where Jesus had been *cropped from the picture* by Rationalism and Individualism. Unfortunately in America, the *Self* has become the center. The customer is King. The target market is Sovereign. Church life has deteriorated to the point that if it is not personally relevant, people will stop attending.

In Part Two, the Traditional, Pragmatic, and Emerging methods were defined as three contemporary versions of *Jesus being cropped from the picture*. Part Three now answers the question: *How can Jesus be restored in the picture?"*

"Jesus and his Kingdom Story" must replace the "individual customer" as **King and Sovereign**. His Kingdom must be reconstituted as the **SUBJECT** of the picture.

The Need for a Constant

In order to re-orient Christians around Christ's Story, there needs to be agreement about that which is *fixed and constant*. Take the weather as an example. People everywhere are accustomed to orienting their behavior *around the weather*. Nobody places themself as sovereign *above the weather*, despite human attempts to control its effects through air conditioning, heating, shelter, and clothing. It is universally understood that the weather cannot be changed or controlled (and oftentimes it cannot even be predicted). People must submit their actions to the seasons and changes in weather.

In the same way, there needs to be something constant in the Church, like the weather, around which Christians everywhere, and at all times, can orient themselves. Webber said:

> The point of integration with a new culture is not to restore that cultural form of Christianity, but to recover the universally accepted framework of faith that originated with the apostles, was developed by the Fathers, and has been handed down by the church in its liturgical and theological traditions. This hermeneutic allows us to face the changing cultural situation with integrity. Our calling is not to reinvent the Christian faith, but, in keeping with the past, to carry forward what the church has affirmed from its beginning.[109]

This framework is the *Constant* that was given by God himself, not formed by human conception or cultural forces. Wells asserted, "The church's goals and functions, therefore, are *given* to it. They come, not from business manuals, not from cultural norms, and not from marketing savvy."[110] Fortunately, the Holy Spirit has given the Church this *Constant* so the Church is not left to her own devices to figure out what to believe.

The Church's Sacred Roots

One of my favorite movies is *Back to the Future*,[111] where Marty (Michael J. Fox) is inadvertently taken back in time to discover the origin of his family and, his friend, Doc Brown. Marty's experience with his past shapes his entire identity upon his return to his own time.

In the same way, churches need to reconnect with their ancient identity, as *People of the Story*. As they *retrieve* the Church's common, sacred roots (Rom. 11.16), they can re-orient themselves around *Christ and his Kingdom Story*, just as humans orient themselves around the weather and the seasons.

Identification with the Church's *Sacred Roots* suggests that Christians must submit to the Holy Spirit's version of the Story in his authorship of the *Scriptures (Canon) and in the formation of the Creeds*, articulated in the first five centuries of the Church.[112] The Holy Spirit guided the Church to spell out what is to believed throughout the centuries. This was done before Postmodernity, Modernity, the Reformation, evangelicalism, or any other cultural or philosophical event. **Apostolic, orthodox, and authoritative faith was given to the Church in the first five centuries, and is called the "Great Tradition"** (not to be confused with the *Traditional Method* which formed 15 centuries later). Dr. Don Davis clarified the significance of the Great Tradition:

> Indeed, the Church of Jesus Christ is the *"People of the Story"*: we are a people birthed, formed, and established by the narrative of God's work in history in the Patriarchs, Israel, and its climax, the incarnation, death, and resurrection of the

Son of God, Jesus of Nazareth. The Great Tradition represents that central core of Christian belief and practice derived from the Scriptures that runs between the time of Christ and the middle of the fifth century. We believe that most of what has proven essential and foundational to Christian theology, spirituality, and witness was articulated by the ancient-undivided Church by the fifth century in its life together, and its canon, creeds, and councils.[113]

<u>The Great Tradition</u>
The Great Tradition represents the Church's historic understanding, articulation, and defense of the Faith, drawn from the **Scriptures** that tell the authoritative Story of God's redemptive plan for the nations, to be accomplished by **Christus Victor**, who carries out the plan through **the universal Church** (God's people throughout the world and throughout time and called to **embody and proclaim** the redemptive Story). Accurate interpretation of this Story is measured by the **Ancient Rule of Faith** ("that which has always been believed, everywhere, and by all") and the **Creeds**, especially the Nicene Creed.[114]

With the articulation of the Great Tradition, Christians have the final and official apostolic message from which to contextualize the gospel in all cultures, throughout time. Webber said, "Jesus Christ [is] the ultimate authority interpreted by the apostles. The Bible is authoritative because it preserves and hands down this witness. The rule of faith and the creeds enjoy a kind of authority because they remain faithful to apostolic tradition. The Holy Spirit 'oversaw' this process so we can speak of Scripture as the revealed and inspired Word of God and the ecumenical creeds as authoritative summaries of the biblical faith."[115]

The Great Tradition is like the great hall that C.S. Lewis mentions in *Mere Christianity*, a hall having many doors opening into different rooms.[116] These rooms represent different church traditions, denominations, and expressions.

Each expression of the Great Tradition should be varied, creative, and flexible, but only *within the confines of what the Holy Spirit has given the Church* in the Great Tradition. The Protestant, Orthodox, and Roman Catholic branches of the Church all came after the Great Tradition, and each branch has continued to affirm it for the last 16 centuries.

Therefore, Christians are not free to disagree with, or reinterpret, the identity and Story of Jesus. His followers must represent the Story as he revealed it, happily submitting to the documents of faith that have been handed down through the Church.

Once anchored to the Great Tradition, a church is free to express itself culturally, liturgically, or theologically, exemplifying the creativity of God himself. Each room, connected to the great hall, is free to design their layout and furnishings in a way that helps them bring glory to Jesus. God's promise to Abraham to include members from every tribe, language, and nation (see Chapter 12) should prompt this kind of joyful pursuit of free expression in Christ.

The results could be hundreds of new movements and expressions of faith, each having an appreciation for one another, rather than living in competition and suspicion. The enemy desires division in the Church, but God desires unity.

Identification with the Church's *Sacred Roots* could provide healing and convergence within the body of Christ (see Figure 18).

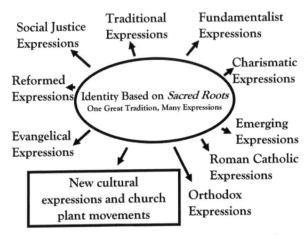

Figure 18: One Great Tradition, Many Expressions

In a world eager to employ a plethora of clever innovations to enhance the Church's image, embracing the Church's *Sacred Roots* stands in stark contrast to various methods to attract people to church, boost attendance, create a new craze, help people feel better about themselves, or return America back to a bygone era. Instead, it is an effort to restore *Jesus as the* **SUBJECT** *of the picture*, reinforce that the Church is the **OBJECT**, and remind Christians that there is an adversarial kingdom in this cosmic Story.

In other words, forging an identity that is based on the Great Tradition is a powerful way to help Jesus' followers resist the tendency to *crop Jesus from the picture*. This is a call for all Christians to become *People of the Story*, an invitation to conform to that which was *given to the Church*, not formed by cultural forces.

Recovering from Fragmentation

One of the most significant cultural influences in recent history is an aspect of the *Marketing Concept* called "target marketing," which gained acceptance in the 1970s and 1980s. In various ways, the Traditional, Pragmatic, and Emerging methods all succumbed to *target marketing,* which follows three major steps:

> The first is *market segmentation,* the act of dividing a market into distinct groups of buyers who might require separate products and/or marketing mixes. The company identifies different ways to segment the market, develops profiles of the market segments, and evaluates each segment's attractiveness. The second step is *market targeting,* the act of evaluating and selecting one or more of the market segments to enter. The third step is *product positioning,* the act of formulating a competitive positioning for the product and a detailed marketing mix.[117]

Churches followed the first step (*market segmentation*) when they segmented their "buyers" into various groups. Some churches *segmented by age,* creating youth programs or establishing adult Christian education groups (Sunday School) based on seasons of life. Some churches segmented over *music preferences* by creating two services (one contemporary, the other traditional). Other churches segmented by offering special programs or activities that meet *specific needs* (financial training, substance abuse), or by *gender interests* (women's or men's ministries). The Emerging church focuses on a specific *cultural* segment of the population (Postmodernity).

Churches employed the second step (*market targeting*) by selecting which groups had the best chance of success in their church. Finally, the third step (*product positioning*) was implemented when programs were designed to suit the segmented groups.

All these segmenting activities were fine on the surface, but without a foundational identity, rooted in the Kingdom Story, segmenting had a disunifying affect on the local church. When churches split people into various affinity groups (segments), each affinity group forms a *sense of identity* that separates it from the church as a whole. Since each local church had already lost its connection to the overall Story *(when Christ was cropped from the picture)*, target marketing in the local church created *another layer of disconnection* from the Story. Identity was no longer grounded in the Kingdom, nor the Church, nor even the local church. Instead, the individuals identified themselves as part of an *affinity group* ("my youth group, my mid-week Bible study, or my adult Sunday School class").

This kind of fragmentation can create multiple "churches within a church," where the local church (church A) is viewed as separate from the affinity group (church B). Each church B may have little to no allegiance to church A except as "A" provides for "B." So a person can be perfectly content to attend an adult Sunday school class without connecting to the broader community (church A) in which it was formed.

De-Cropping by Un-Segmenting

Where the *Marketing Concept* seeks to separate people into segments based on personal interests, identification with the Church's *Sacred*

Roots <u>consolidates</u> Christians into a common identity. Personal *choice* gives way to common *identity*.

Every affinity group within the church can be "unsegmented" by re-orienting around "the Story." Each Christian can pledge allegiance to the Story, trumping their loyalty to their affinity group. They can understand their identity in light of the Story revealed in the Great Tradition.

In other words, all Christians must see themselves as *People of the Story* (1 Pet. 2.9-10). This is the Story given in the Great Tradition, a *gift to the Church Universal, through the Scriptures, summarized in the Creeds, and understood through the lens of the Ancient Rule of Faith, achieved by Christus Victor, so the gospel goes to all nations, for the fulfillment of God's purposes.*

The Story, expressed in the Great Tradition, has been given to the Church by the Holy Spirit. It is not invented—it is entrusted to God's people and God expects his followers to submit themselves to it. This is the Story around which all Christians, traditions, denominations, and affinity groups must orient their lives. To defy the Great Tradition is to be outside Christian faith.[118]

Although Americans cannot escape a self-oriented culture, they do not have to be governed by the *Marketing Concept.* Churches can choose to be *People of the Story* by refusing the cultural pressure of target marketing.

Chapter 18: *Sacred Roots:* **Not Culturally Formed**

FORMING AN IDENTITY based on the Church's *Sacred Roots* can be understood by contrasting it to the Traditional, Pragmatic, and Emerging methods in terms of previously-mentioned categories: Cultural Assumptions, Nostalgic Era, Common Antagonists, and Focus of Energy. This chapter will focus on *cultural assumptions*.

Sacred Roots is not a cultural development like Rationalism, the *Marketing Concept*, or Postmodernity, but that which was **given** to the Church by the Holy Spirit, articulated in the Great Tradition. This pre-dates America, Frontier Revivalism, Modernity, evangelicalism, the Reformation, and all the other cultural manifestations by which other methods were formed.

During the first five centuries of the Church, Christian faith was articulated as the Church was guided by the Holy Spirit. Despite the cultural contexts and worldviews of the early Church fathers, the work of God, articulated in the Great Tradition, has stood the test of time and has been embraced by the Church ever since.

Sacred Roots is neither Modern nor Postmodern, nor does it focus on any one particular cultural expression. The *People of the Story* seek to restore what was *cropped from the picture*. Therefore, churches who identify with these *Sacred Roots* are empowered to contextualize the Great Tradition in cultures around the world.

Jesus Cropped from the Picture

More Than Cultural Rationalism

For the first centuries of the Church, the Story had a strong *narrative* emphasis. However, with the wholesale acceptance of Rationalism, appreciation for the narrative quality of Scripture diminished. A renewed commitment to its *Sacred Roots* can liberate churches from their cultural limitations by re-discovering a narrative view of the Scriptures.

Every epic story and fairy tale is simply a *shadow of the big Story of Christ and his Kingdom.* Every culture has its mythology because it represents the larger cosmic Story. This is why Ecclesiastes says God "has put eternity into man's heart" (Eccles. 3.11).

Such larger-than-life stories have the same elements: love, danger, heroism, romance, sacrifice, good versus evil, unlikely heroes, insurmountable odds, a fellowship, hope from beyond that pulls people through at the end. These stories follow the same story line: things were good, then something awful happened; now a great battle must take place to put things right, and a hero must come at the last minute to save the day.[119] This pattern is also present in every movie that touches people profoundly:

- Aslan is on the move to rescue Narnia.
- Dorothy must find a way home.
- Luke Skywalker must help Obi-Wan Kenobi defeat the Empire.
- Gepetto must be found at sea.
- The town must rally to George Bailey's aid.
- The kids have to find a way to get ET home.
- Mr. Smith is compelled to filibuster in Washington.
- Rick must let Elsa go to escape the Nazis.
- The Fellowship of the Ring must destroy the ring of power.
- Atticus Finch must represent the falsely accused.

In his Story, Jesus goes to heroic lengths to win the day and calls his followers to do the same. Epic stories provide people with a broader vision so they can escape "this provincial life."

Brian Cavanaugh said, "Stories, parables, fables, anecdotes, illustrations, etc., help us to see the 'bigger picture' in life. They help us to understand there is more to life than our own limited spheres of experience. They create pictures in our mind and open up our imagination to comprehend a greater dimension of life than we are normally used to experiencing. Stories are vehicles that take us to far off places, places we've never experienced ourselves."[120]

More Bible, Not Less

The Traditional Method may respond negatively to the idea of Truth as "Story." For them, the word "Story" demeans the veracity of the Scriptures, reducing God's Word to something trivial or mythical. Traditionals may even erroneously infer that embracing *Sacred Roots* shows allegiance with liberalism. Actually, the opposite is true. Adopting a narrative approach provides Christians with *more Bible* teaching, not *less.*

When the Scriptures become an owner's manual for *my personal relationship to Christ*, the Word of God is no longer the authoritative Truth, but a superficial list of "do's and don'ts" that can be accepted, or rejected, at any time. To describe it as "Story" simply means that Scripture's authority is broad and comprehensive, beyond "how it applies to me."

Those who reject a narrative approach repeat the mistake of mid-20th century liberal theologians like Rudolf Bultmann. His classic argument was that the New Testament story of salvation made no sense to a Modern mind. Bultmann said the Bible needed to be stripped of the husk of myth (Story) in order to get to the kernel of truth (Rationalism).[121] By so doing, Bultmann essentially *cropped Jesus' Story from the picture*. Ironically, when Traditionals reject a narrative view, they are in danger of the same liberal errors they originally organized to combat.

A New Way of Presenting

Adopting a narrative view is much more than showing video clips in church services or incorporating a more visually-oriented environment in the sanctuary, as helpful as those steps might be.

Pastors, elders, deacons, teens, and adults must be re-oriented to a narrative understanding of the Bible, which may not provide the "direct application" many have been trained to crave. Teachers must learn to resist the urge to give a moral application with every teaching. *Moralism, factualism, and particularism* (see Chapter 11) need to be resisted in favor of the Bible's redemptive Story. This requires a re-evaluation of the entire mindset of children's curriculum, follow-up and discipleship materials, and Sunday school programs.

As a result, teachers should reconsider a spectator format that utilizes linguistic, linear presentations that appeal to audience's minds; the "how-to in seven easy steps" approach. Instead, every lesson should be a sub-story of the larger Story. The use of story and metaphor can be more than just a "hook" to capture the listener's interest, but become the actual "meat" of the presentation.

With the Story as the centerpiece of every teaching, the *past, present, and future work of Christ to overcome the powers of evil* should be implicit in each gathering, whether large or small. Without a transparent connection to the Story of Christ's Kingdom work, the teaching should be re-considered until such connections are obvious. Repeated declaration of this global context is the best way to ground new believers in the faith and help veterans avoid *cropping Jesus from the picture*.

The Urban Church Advantage
Around the world, the church among the poor is growing, in part because the poor operate in a pre-Modern mindset that is open to narrative. They never *cropped Jesus from the picture* to fit a pre-conceived self-orientation. The Bible's Story can be quickly integrated into the church's life when it does not have to be translated through a *Western Rationalistic* and *Individualistic* paradigm.

America's urban poor have not always embraced Modernity as an ally because it was often seen as a *source of their misery*. Those who became powerful in Modernity often used their power to oppress the poor. So endless debates about Postmodernity are for those who have enough leisure time to engage in such philosophical discussions. The poor do not care about the Modern-Postmodern arguments between Traditionals and Emergings. In fact, the poor can proceed unencumbered from such cultural distractions, focusing on Christ and his Kingdom, as the *People of the Story*. The shortcomings of the Traditional, Pragmatic, and Emerging methods can be avoided like plague-infested villages.

Jesus Cropped from the Picture

A Multi-Dimensional View of Atonement

The *People of the Story* can reject the pressure to choose among any of the one-dimensional views of the atonement, most of which are shaped by cultural attempts to contextualize the gospel. The various one-dimensional views of the atonement are too small to capture the fullness of Jesus' work when each is considered by itself.

Those who are shaped by *Sacred Roots* recognize *all* the multiple victories of Christus Victor: his incarnation, triumph over temptation, miracles of exorcism and healing, sinless life and example, authoritative commissioning of the apostles, death, resurrection, ascension, current intercession, and future return. While the Cross is still Jesus' central, crowning achievement, the other aspects of Christ's victory over the powers of evil should not minimized, but celebrated.

The Great Tradition understanding is that *all* of the great works of Christ are part of a **single action to destroy the works of the devil.** The Story is rooted in Christ's determination to win back what was lost at the fall by putting the adversary away forever. Once that overarching theme is understood, the various aspects of the atonement can be appreciated without having to choose one as more important than another.

The picture can be restored by renewing an appreciation for a narrative view of the Scriptures and celebrating the multiple acts of atoning heroism carried out by the Lord and Savior, Jesus Christ.

Chapter 19: *Sacred Roots:* No Nostalgia, No Antagonists

FOR THE TRADITIONAL, Pragmatic, and Emerging methods, nostalgic eras were formed in conjunction with their common antagonists. Traditionals have the Protestant Reformation, Pragmatics recall a personally fulfilling season of life, and Emergings idealize the early Church before Constantine.

However, the *People of the Story* have no specific nostalgic era. There is no "classic era" where the Church was operating in its fullness. There is no "golden age" to long for or reminisce about. In every era, the Church has made mistakes in representing Christ. Despite her mistakes, the Holy Spirit has continued to be at work in the Church *in every era*, and the gates of hell have not prevailed against his Kingdom advance.

Furthermore, the Church is "catholic" (universal) because it is made up of *all* believers past, present, and future. This view of the Church allows Christians of *all* expressions to claim *all* of the Church's victories as their own. Billy Graham, Susanna Wesley, Martin Luther, Thomas Aquinas, Patrick, Augustine, Francis of Assisi, John of the Cross, and Paul of Tarsus are all part of the company to which every follower of Jesus belongs. *All* the saints of God belong to *one another*.

Those who are anchored to *Sacred Roots* do not long for an idyllic *past*, but a perfect *future*. There is no "safety of the Shire" as longed for in *Lord of the Rings*. Instead, the Church age is a "battle for Middle Earth" and is full of destruction and disharmony. But the battle is worth fighting because of certain victory through the Lord Jesus. Christians should long for home in the presence of God, not a trip back to some past earthly glory.

Defining Period

The *People of the Story* appreciate the Holy Spirit's at work in all the eras of the Church: Biblical, Ancient, Medieval, Reformation, Modern, and Postmodern (see Appendix 5, "Six Paradigms of History"). It may appear that the Ancient era (100-451) is idealized, as though the Ancients were more pure in their devotion than in other times. This is not the case.

However, what is noteworthy about this period is that *God the Holy Spirit* led the Church to articulate, once and for all, the foundational beliefs and practices that have persisted throughout the Church Age. God's work to establish the Great Tradition was a defining act that has empowered the Church to keep its footing for the last 1600 years. Those basic beliefs and practices of Christian faith will continue to guide the Church until Jesus returns.

All that now remains is to declare the gospel of the Kingdom and embody the Great Tradition among all people groups on earth.

No Common Antagonists

While the Traditional, Pragmatic, and Emerging methods react to their own antagonists, the *People of the Story* have no common cultural antagonists. There is no desperation regarding Modernity, Postmodernity, secularism, loss of American influence, rise in multi-culturalism, illegal immigration, liberalism, Roman Catholicism, or even the advance of

Islam or the cults. They encourage vigorous debate with those inside and outside the Christian faith, but not from the standpoint of despair, but rather with the Kingdom's posture of "righteousness and peace and joy in the Holy Spirit (Rom. 14.17)."

The reason for this confidence is the inevitability of God's future victory (Matt. 16.18). All cultures, traditions, and philosophies will one day be subsumed or destroyed by "the Kingdom of our Lord and of his Christ. And he shall reign forever and ever (Rev. 11.15)." Pastors need not fear a decline in church attendance, a flagging budget, nor losing prestige among their peers. When Christians focus on the continuing victory of Christ, there is no need for insecurity, because the *People of the Story* are overcomers (Rom. 8.37-39).

The Real Antagonists

Christ's Kingdom is not of this world (John 18.36), so the antagonists in the Story are not flesh and blood, but the rulers, authorities, and cosmic powers of darkness (Eph. 6.12). Christians resist the devil[122] and his oppressive kingdom which sets itself against the Kingdom of God. The devil is a real adversary with nefarious plots against Christ and his creation. All of the many wicked atrocities of genocide, child prostitution, torture, and terrorism have been designed by Satan and his minions.

In addition to the devil, the Bible also spells out two other sources of evil and pain: the world[123] and the flesh.[124] The *world* is the fallen system of nature and humanity that wreaks havoc, misery, and toil on the universe. People get sick and die. Equipment and homes fall into disrepair. People create systems of greed, lust, and pride that oppress others and enslave themselves. God's goodness is twisted into ugliness.

The *flesh* is the sin nature that prompts people to rebel against God and join the enemy. Anything evil or unpleasant, causing tears and dread, can find its source in the *devil, the world, or the flesh.*

Kingdom warfare is broader than engagement with sentient spiritual beings. Spiritual warfare is threefold: there are *supernatural battles* against the <u>devil</u>, social battles against the <u>world</u>'s brokenness, and *personal battles* against the <u>flesh</u>.[125] These three are the *true* antagonists against which Jesus' followers are to fight.

Suffering

Jesus was *cropped from the picture* in part because his antagonists (devil, world, flesh) were cropped from it as well. Therefore, the de-cropping process involves putting evil and suffering back in the picture. The existence of the devil, world, and flesh makes it clear that the *Kingdom is about conflict.* Since Jesus came to destroy the works of the devil (1 John 3.8) and win back that which was lost (Luke 19.10), it is natural that Ed Murphy would say, "the normal Christian life is lived in the context of on-going spiritual warfare. To receive Christ is to enlist."[126] W. Russell Maltby said, "Jesus promised His disciples three things: that they would be entirely fearless, absurdly happy, and that they would get into trouble."[127]

Since the Church is at war against the kingdom of this world, no one should be surprised by casualties (1 Pet. 4.12, 5.8-10). "As Jesus'

Kingdom advances, the forces of evil will only intensify their futile attempts to destroy it."[128] Jesus himself commanded his people to be faithful, even to the point of death (Rev. 2.10). There are no guarantees that Christians will be exempt from trouble, hardship, divisions, persecution, or even martyrdom (Rom. 8.35). In fact, the New Testament promises his people should expect every kind of trial (James 1.2, 1 Thess. 3.2-3).

Therefore, Christianity is not a formula that ensures success and blessing. John White said, "Of course you may get wounded in battle! Of course you may get knocked off your feet! But it is the man or woman who gets up and fights again that is a true warrior. There is no place for giving up. The warfare is so much bigger than your personal humiliations. To feel sorry for oneself is totally inappropriate. Over such a soldier I would pour a bucket of icy water. I would drag him to his feet, kick him in the rear end and put his sword in his hand and shout,'Now fight!'"[129]

Say It Ain't So!
One may hope to avoid spiritual conflict, but that is wishful thinking. In the *Lord of the Rings: The Two Towers*, Aragorn admonished King Theoden to muster his troops for battle against the invading army. When Theoden hesitated, not wanting to risk open war, Aragorn wisely admonished him that open war *was upon him*, whether Theoden liked it or not.

Some people wish to deny the devil's existence. Others feel un-comfortable with the idea of confronting the influence of his kingdom (devil, world, flesh). They may think, "Perhaps if we do not confront evil, we can escape difficulty. Why stir up trouble when the powers of evil are defeated in the end anyway? Let's not provoke them. Let sleeping dogs lie."

Certainly, it is unwise to provoke or taunt the enemy (Jude 9), but leaving the powers of evil alone will not exempt anyone from trials. Such naivete about the enemy's schemes ignores the fact that there are beings who attack at their own initiative and with ruthless persistence (2 Cor. 2.11). This kind of thinking leaves believers vulnerable to disillusionment and ineffective in a crisis. They can be caught off guard when tribulation strikes.

One's illusions about spiritual warfare will not change the reality of it. This conflict has been raging long before anyone was born and will go on long into the future, until Jesus comes to end it once and for all. It is not a war any human started and no human will end it. Ignoring it and hoping it goes away will have no effect. The powers of evil will not relent simply because people avoid them.

Weapons for Battle
Fortunately, God has not left his people defenseless against the world, the flesh, and the devil. He has provided weapons for this warfare (2 Cor. 10.4). The Word of God provides truth, comfort, wisdom, instruction, and encouragement (2 Tim. 3.15-17, Heb. 5.14, James 1.22-25, Rom. 15.4). There is an entire set of armor to help the believer fight off confusion, distraction, lies, temptations, doubts, and accusations (Eph. 6.10-18).

The Holy Spirit comforts and guides believers as they wage the good warfare together, provides gifted shepherds to protect and mobilize the army, and prompts people to "count it all joy" whenever various trials are encountered (1 Tim. 1.18, Eph. 4.11-13, James 1.2, Rom. 5.1-5). There can be joy in the midst of pain because God can sovereignly redeem every trial, changing it into a victory against the enemy's kingdom. What the devil means for ill, God can turn to good (Gen. 50.20, Heb. 12.3-15).

While the devil desires God's people to give up in discouragement, shame, or guilt, God desires his people to fight back by pressing on, "getting back into the game." Jesus' victory over the devil pays for sin, so Christians do not have to entertain the persistent accusations of the enemy. Baptism is a weapon for battle in that it is a concrete reminder of allegiance to the Victorious Christ and his Kingdom, despite how defeated one feels (Acts 26.17-18, Mark 16.15-16, Rom. 6.3-23). When under attack, Luther often exclaimed, "I am baptized!"

These weapons provide courage in the face of trying circumstances, forgiveness in spite of failure, and a *will to win* when everything seems hopeless. Christ's guaranteed victory over Satan carries his people through, despite the onslaught of the devil, the world, and the flesh (1 Cor. 10.13). Believers are instructed to meet together regularly in order to remember their destiny and hope (Heb. 10.25). Because of the human tendency to forget, the celebration of communion is a frequent reminder, not only of Jesus' past death, but of his future victory, consummated at the Wedding Banquet of the Lamb (Mark 14.25). As John White said:

Indeed we fight a war which is already won. It was won when Jesus burst from a sealed tomb. In World War 2 when the allies invaded Europe, the whole world knew that the war was really over. Months of death and bitter fighting lay ahead. There would be cold and exhaustion, peril, and pain, the crumple of bombs and the sickening death-swoops of flaming aircraft. But the end had really come.... We are now in precisely the same position. The last invasion is on. 'In the world,' stated Jesus, 'you have tribulation, but be of good cheer, I *have* overcome the world' (John. 16.33).... Now there are times when you feel anything but like a member of a triumphant army. You will feel alone, small, weak. The battle therefore is also essentially a battle of *faith*.[130]

The Search for Causes

The Rationalistic mind desires to find a *cause and effect* for every trial. It is assumed that if the source can be discovered, a solution can be applied and the trial ended or avoided. But this is not the way of the Kingdom. God often chooses to conceal the cause of trials, as he did with Job, and prefers that his followers trust he is coordinating everything to accomplish his Kingdom plan. For those who are called according to his purpose (Rom. 8.28), there will be frequent times when there is no apparent reason for the tribulation they experience.

But whether the source of pain is the devil, the world, or the flesh, *the answer is always the same*: trust Christ to accomplish his Kingdom work. No one needs to know if sickness or death is caused by the devil, personal sin, or because the person lives in a germ-filled world. Searching for the cause is often a waste of energy. Trusting in

Christ is the best solution because it frees the suffering person from searching for an answer that may never be revealed. Instead of frantic efforts to find out "why," believers who suffer should "entrust their souls to a faithful Creator while doing good" (1 Pet. 4.19).

Building an identity based on *Sacred Roots* will de-crop the picture so that both *Jesus and the powers of evil* are restored to the picture. A proper understanding of the *devil, the world, and the flesh* is vital for Christians to understand the reality of the conflict around them, allowing them to be restored to vibrant faith.

Chapter 20: *Sacred Roots*: **Focus of Energy**

RATHER THAN GOING back to glory days (Traditional), reacting to shifting market conditions (Pragmatic), or contextualizing within a single culture (Emerging), energy should be directed toward **integrating personal and community faith activities around the Story of Christ's Kingdom, articulated by the Great Tradition.** Every aspect of local church life must be de-segmented, re-oriented, and re-integrated back to a single theme: allegiance to *Christ and his Kingdom Story.* The goal is to restore Jesus' prominence so he is not *cropped out of the picture.*

Appreciating Local Tradition

In Chapter 17, the Great Tradition was described as a Story (Scriptures) of a Champion (Christus Victor) who forms a People (Church) who are called to re-enact, embody, and continue the Story, narrated by the Holy Spirit (Creeds and Rule of Faith). The Great Tradition is the authoritative foundation for *all* Christians, of *all* traditions, for *all* time. These are the elements that need to be incorporated in every dimension of a church's life. But in addition to the Great Tradition, each church should understand and appreciate *its own legacy of faith.*

For example, Baptists should make their Baptist distinctives known. Lutherans should tell their family history. Foursquare congregations should ensure an appreciation of their own spiritual tradition. Every congregation should not only affirm its commitment to the Great Tradition, but also explain its unique place within the Church.

Because the *People of the Story* seek a variety of expressions, the existence of denominations need not be an embarrassment. In fact, denominations can be viewed as an expression of the creative work of the Holy Spirit. "Different denominations with their distinct theological traditions are a means whereby God leads us corporately to wrestle through understanding truth. Our differences are things that haven't been settled yet."[131] Integration based on *Sacred Roots* does not mean not the assimilation of all Christian traditions into one institutional form, devoid of denominational distinctives. The Church is "One" because of its common commitments to Christ and his Kingdom, as articulated in the Great Tradition, not because denominations shed themselves all of uniqueness.

The *People of the Story* can grow in their appreciation for the unity *and* diversity of the Church by studying other traditions and expressions of faith throughout Church history (Richard Foster's *Streams of Living Water*[132] is a helpful introduction).

Dimensions of Integration

As a church seeks to embody its *Sacred Roots*, four dimensions of application can be considered: *theology, worship, discipleship,* and *outreach.*

One way to conceptualize these categories is through the Great Commandment to love God and love one's neighbor (Matt. 22.37-40). In other words, *theology* is the Church's reflection on the nature of God, *worship* is the expression of love for God, *outreach* is the outpouring of love toward others, and *discipleship* is the process of increasing a believer's capacity to *theologize, worship, and do outreach.*

These suggestions are not meant to be prescriptive:

⋄ **Theology** is the Church's *reflection on the Story of God's Kingdom victory over the devil*, revealed in the Great Tradition. With humility, believers look to God's inspired Word, the councils and creeds, and the history of the Church to understand this triumphant Story, so the *People of the Story* can re-enact, embody, and continue the Story. The Church's *worship, discipleship,* and *outreach* grow out of its theology, expressed in various ways among orthodox traditions.

⋄ **Worship**[133] can be thought of in terms of *frustrating the kingdom of darkness by declaring the excellence of our God and King* (John 4.24). This includes individual and corporate expressions of devotion for the glory of God, not for the accomplishment of any outreach or benefit to self or others.[128] Worship includes singing, prayer, and the spiritual disciplines. While believers profit from these activities, they are done out of love for God, not for the welfare of the individual.

⋄ **Discipleship** equips believers *to join the battle against the other kingdom* (Matt. 28.18-20, 2 Tim. 2.2). Children and new adult believers must be oriented to their new identity as the *People of the Story*. Then they must continually grow in their ability to represent the Kingdom. This occurs through a variety of creative ways including preaching, Bible studies, drama, the sacraments, informal meetings, formal catechism, children's education, small groups, Sunday School, and confirmation classes.

⬦ **Outreach** is the *declaration and demonstration of the gospel to carry on the work of Christ to destroy the enemy's works* (Acts 8.26-40, Luke 4.18-19, Titus 2.11-14, Matt. 24.14, 2 Pet. 3.12). Outreach includes acts of compassion, proclamation of the gospel message, and sending missionaries across cultures to plant new churches. Christians accomplish outreach when they invite people to follow Jesus and join the Church, but they also do outreach when they perform works of justice, freedom, and wholeness, independent of whether the gospel is proclaimed or accepted. Christians do good works because of God's heart. The Church's legacy of meeting human needs through education, health care, clean water, and orphanages are a few of the examples of Christ's prediction that the Church would do greater works than Christ (John 14.12). These acts of kindness do violence to the kingdom of Satan (Matt. 11.12).

The *People of the Story* continually grow in Christlike *discipleship* as they *worship*, increase in their understanding of *theology,* and do *outreach.* Each person exercises their spiritual gifts as their church opposes the other kingdom.

While the Traditional and Pragmatic methods emphasize "the church gathered (church happens inside)," and the Emerging Method focuses on "the church dispersed (church happens outside)," the *People of the Story* seek a more holistic approach that recognizes the church both *gathered and dispersed.* In theology, worship, discipleship, and outreach, Christians work out their salvation individually *and* corporately, making the local church a community that gathers and disperses (see Chapter 8) in a natural cycle of life; week-to-week, season-to-season, and year-to-year.

Identification with the Church's *Sacred Roots* is not the pursuit of a method. Methods prompt questions like, "Is it working? Are they coming? Are they fed? Is it relevant to Postmodernity?" The better question is, **"Are we faithful to the Story in all aspects of our life together?"** If so, a church can be free from methodological anxieties.

Christians are restored to vibrant faith when churches focus their personal and community energy around the Church's *Sacred Roots*—as *People of the Story*.

Chapter 21: Becoming *People of the Story*

THE STORY IS God's unfolding drama, where the **Father is the Author, Jesus is the Champion, and the Holy Spirit is the Narrator, told through the Bible, the Great Tradition, and Church history.** God invites all people to join this ancient drama, and all who respond by faith are grafted into this identity. They become *People of the Story.*

Christians have received this identity from the Church, who received it from the apostles, who received it from Jesus, who received it from the Father. Such identity spells out what Christians believe, who they are, where they came from, where they are going, and what they should do.

A Branch of the Tree

Instead of a collection of individuals, gathering around a common philosophy, a church must understand itself like a branch of a tree that grows up from its *Sacred Roots*. This is why *Sacred Roots* is symbolized by a tree (see Figure 19).

Figure 19: *Sacred Roots*

My friend, Brad Brown, extended this metaphor:

> He is the Vine, you are the branches! Which gives us a deep, enriching connection—a bond with other Christians city-wide, state-wide, nation-wide, world-wide! Parts of every culture and race ... connected to the One, True Vine since time began. Thousands upon thousands of limbs, branches, shoots, saplings, twigs and leaves getting their sustenance and support from a forever Source that is deeply rooted in eternity. And it is from this gigantic, ancient trunk twisting and turning down through history, that the Creator has cultivated an incredible, multitudinous variety of millions and millions of fruit that have blossomed and burst forth beyond the wildest dreams and expectations of our agricultural limitations and individual imaginations.[134]

Those who want to become the *People of the Story* must make a wholesale commitment to this comprehensive shift in identity. It is not practical to "tinker around the edges," or "gradually move in that direction." Rationalism, *The Marketing Concept*, Postmodernity, or any number of cultural factors will continually pull a church off course unless there is consensus among the leadership to break free from its gravitational pull.

Churches must correlate all aspects of church life to the Story. Don Davis said:

The Story shapes our family and body life:

⬦ In *theology*, we affirm God as the Author of the Story, Jesus of Nazareth as its Champion, and the Holy Spirit as the interpreter of the Story.

⬦ *The Scriptures* are the living testimony and record of the Story.

⬦ In our *worship* we historically recite the Story, prophetically proclaim the Story, and dramatically reenact the Story.

⬦ In *initiation and incorporation* into our fellowship, we *baptize the converted*, helping them to identify with and embrace the Story.

⬦ In *our discipleship* we learn the Story, memorize and meditate on the Story, and are trained in the meaning of the Story.

⬦ In *spiritual formation* we embody the Story.

⬦ In *counseling and soul care*, we enable others to understand their own life stories in juxtaposition to God's Story.

⬦ In our *service and outreach,* we express the Story's meaning through acts of hospitality and generosity.

⬦ In our *witness* we *proclaim and announce* the Good News of the Story to all who have never heard of God's great Drama.

⬦ In our *hope* we await the consummation and fulfillment of the Story.[135]

Every aspect of the church's activities, programs, structures, and strategies must be evaluated in light of its contribution to the Story. While the Pragmatic Method evaluates based on attendance, giving, and other business-related approaches, the *People of the Story* measure in terms of **faithfulness to the Story**, articulated in the Great Tradition. Since this may be a new way of thinking about ministry, it may take considerable practice.

Activity Evaluation

As a starting point, every affinity group (see Chapter 17) and every program or activity must be eligible for consideration (see Figure 20).

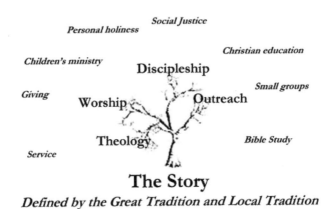

The Story
Defined by the Great Tradition and Local Tradition

Figure 20: Activity Evaluation

Then, that activity must be evaluated in terms of its connection to the Story of Christ and his Kingdom, as an expression of either theology, worship, discipleship, or outreach.

The first evaluation question is **"Does this activity help our congregation increase our capacity to theologize, worship, disciple, and do outreach, or is it designed to increase attendance?"** Activities designed to "increase attendance" or "meet people's felt needs," should be viewed with suspicion, and considered for elimination or adjustment. For example, a six-week study on personal finances should not be to *help people manage their finances better* but to *increase their capacity* to steward their finances for greater Kingdom <u>outreach</u>.

A second question is, **"Does this activity help our congregation understand the Story in a deeper way or does it reinforce some aspect that crops Jesus from the picture?"** Activities that reinforce SLIM assumptions might be counter-productive to the health of the participants. For example, a small group Bible study that meets to study books that emphasize a *Substitute Center* may be locking its members "in a SLIM prison" (see Chapter 11). It may be better for the small group to reconsider their study materials rather than risk continued exposure to the *SLIMming Effect.*

A third question is, **"Does this activity use Target Marketing to segment the congregation, or does it promote a sense of loyalty to the Church Universal and the local church?"** For example, does the women's Bible study have its own sense of identity apart from the local church, or are the women consistently aware of their connection to the whole? Perhaps it has it become its own affinity group (church B).

Every dimension of church life must embody, re-enact, and express the Story through theology, worship, discipleship, and outreach. The process of target marketing can be reversed through a re-integration around the Story. Therefore, children, teens, adults, men's and women's ministries, small groups, substance abuse groups, counseling ministries, elder and deacon boards, Bible studies, Sunday school classes, and short-term mission teams all must see themselves in light of the Story.

Developing an identity, as *People of the Story,* is a process that can occur at the simplest levels. For example a faithful nursery worker, who lovingly holds babies each week, is doing powerful Kingdom work. The baby's parents are freed up for worship and the child experiences the security of being loved by an extended family of faith. Without saying a word, the tender servant of God is passing on a sense of identity to the infant. This process, reinforced by hundreds of encounters with people in the church throughout childhood, cements an identity based on the Church's *Sacred Roots*.

The roots of identity deepen through dozens of sidewalk conversations, fellowship activities, retreats, and shared meals. Becoming *People of the Story* is developed slowly over time in relationship with one another, not formally launched as a program or initiative.

Once this process of identity begins to take root, Christians must continually remind one another that the *Story is the center, not the individual*. Such re-orientation must be done in community because of the human tendency to forget. One of the primary duties of a pastor is the ministry of "remembrance."

The goal of Activity evaluation is to *integrate personal and community faith around the Story of Christ and his Kingdom*. Before bored Christians can be restored to vibrant faith, all activities, programs, and strategies must align with the Kingdom Story so *Jesus regains his place as the* SUBJECT. Difficult decisions will have to be made with sensitivity and love, making sure unity is maintained so the enemy cannot gain a foothold through division. However, church leaders need to be bold and courageous to ensure Jesus is not *cropped from the picture*.

Activity evaluation is an effective way to begin the process of forming the church's identity as *People of the Story*. Although these approaches will not ensure increased church attendance or balanced budgets, they will promote Christ as the prominent figure in the church's life, leading to deeper faithfulness and commitment to him.

Chapter 22: More Identity, Less Method

IDENTITY IS A powerful force. The Jewish people had identity as the people of God. They had a family history that connected them to God, with centuries of stories about heroic feats of faith, as well as dismal acts of cowardice (sometimes by the same people). This deep-rooted identity allowed the Church to be established as a continuation of that history. The Gentiles could be grafted into the tree because there were already roots that went deep into the ground of history.

When the roots of identity are shallow, Christians can become confused about who they are, where they came from, and where they are going. When this happens, they often revert to methods, which is why the Traditional, Pragmatic, and Emerging methods have become so popular. Throughout history, when the Church has forgotten its *Sacred Roots*, methods have been emphasized, resulting in *Jesus being cropped from the picture.*

By finding identity in the Story, a church can stay clear of the perils of the Traditional, Pragmatic, and Emerging methods (see Figure 21). Also, with a few adjustments, the Traditional, Pragmatic, and Emerging methods can retain many of their positive qualities and continue to enjoy their distinct practices and heritage.

Liberating The Traditional Method

The primary difficulty for Traditionals is to realize they can embrace the Great Tradition without being disloyal to their commitments to *the Bible and the Cross*. In other words, embracing the Church's *Sacred Roots*

Assumptions	*Identity Based on Sacred Roots*
Starting Point	The Great Tradition
Cultural assumptions	No cultural assumptions
Foundational principle	The Kingdom of God
Era of nostalgia	No nostalgic era
Common antagonist	The world, the flesh, and the devil
Biblical lens	Rational <u>and</u> narrative
Subject/object	Subject: Christ; Object: The Church
Focus of energy	Integrate around the Story
Slogan	Be faithful to the Story

Figure 21: An Identity Based On *Sacred Roots*

is not an act of evangelical apostasy. The *People of the Story* do not ally themselves with any of the Traditionals' common antagonists, but simply seek a retrieval of the Great Tradition that pre-dates all these antagonists.

In fact, identification with *Sacred Roots* is a call for a *greater* emphasis on the Bible than the Traditionals' SLIM approach. Traditionals can rejoice in their devotion to Scripture, knowing there is even *more* to the Word than they originally thought.

A narrative view of the Bible, added to their Rationalistic/Modern view of Scripture, will only enhance their appreciation of the Scriptures. Those who embrace *Sacred Roots* can "have their cake and eat it too." However, it may be difficult to give up their verse-by-verse analysis of the Bible. Reading the Bible with an openness to mystery may be challenging.

Narrative Approach

In order to be effective in cross-cultural mission, Traditionals must broaden their Rationalistic view of the Scriptures to include an appreciation for hearing the Bible as Story. Sometimes Traditionals equate Christian maturity to a SLIM (Linguistic-Mental) educational style, mislabeling New Testament churches as "learning communities." However, during most of its history the Church has learned about Christ through story-telling and metaphor, so a cognitive approach to the Bible must not be the primary means to disciple believers. Traditionals with a heart for the Great Commission must be sensitive to cultures who process information in a narrative way.

View of the Atonement

The Traditionals' one-dimensional view of the atonement, focusing on Jesus' work on the cross, can be retained as the central achievement of Jesus's life. The good news is, there is even *more* to celebrate besides the cross (for personal salvation). The Christus Victor view, rejoicing in all the victories Christ brought against the kingdom of the powers of evil, releases Traditionals to worship Jesus in even more meaningful ways.

Embracing the Pre-Reformation

Another challenge will be the acceptance of anything pre-Reformation, without lessening an appreciation for the Reformation era. It is sometimes difficult to realize the Roman Catholic Church pre-dated Protestantism, and the Great Tradition came before the Roman Catholic Church. For many Traditionals, there is not much of value between the Biblical era and the Reformation. Traditionals miss a wealth of wisdom and insight from men and women who left a legacy of their Christian experience between 100-1500 A.D.

Also, some Traditionals cannot get past the shocking ways the Roman Catholic Church abused its power, falling victim to the surrounding culture during the Medieval era. In their own way, medieval Catholicism *cropped Jesus from the picture*. In fact, any church is susceptible to *cropping Jesus from the picture* by making some aspect of faith the new "method."

While current Roman Catholic practices should be carefully reviewed and evaluated, it should now be clear that the Traditional, Pragmatic, and Emerging methods have also succumbed to their own cultural forces. This is an example where the *log has to be removed from one's own eye* before taking the splinter from the Roman Catholic Church. The Great Tradition provides a safe starting place for loving debate with the Roman Catholic and Eastern Orthodox branches of the Church.

Pressure to Have Answers
Another benefit of embracing the Church's *Sacred Roots* is that the Traditionals' fear of secularism and other philosophies can melt away as they consider making the *world, the flesh, and the devil* their new antagonist. It is no longer necessary to labor under the constant threat of needing Rationalistic answers to every skeptical question.

While the faith should always be vigorously contended (Jude 3), Traditionals can enjoy the freedom of knowing they no longer have to be world-class philosophers to represent Christ effectively. Instead, they can return to a time when people were asked to "believe" first, and "understand the Scriptures" second.

Rationalism suggests people must *understand* before they believe, putting the burden on the person making the argument. But as Webber said, "One must come to the Christian faith believing that it is true and embrace it as such without any dependence on data outside the faith. Christianity requires trust, a believing embrace, a willingness to step inside its story apart from any dependence on historical, scientific, or rational persuasion."[136]

Fortunately, there *are* solid answers for people with genuine questions, but the answers are simple, and can be learned by illiterate people, even children. For example, one piece of evidence is the centuries-long perseverance of One Church (despite her flaws), demonstrated by her commitment to Great Tradition. God's preservation of the Jewish people also confirms his existence. The life, miracles, and resurrection of Christ, revealed in the Scriptures, are a compelling metanarrative that welcomes every culture to join his Story. For those who *want* to believe, there is a mountain of good scientific and philosophical apologetics for virtually every objection ever raised. But for those who choose unbelief, *no amount of evidence will ever be enough.*

Therefore, people do not have to be won by clever argumentation but can simply be invited to *follow Jesus.* If they do not believe, it is not due to the Traditionals' failure to respond to complex and Rationalistic questions; it is the **hearer's** refusal to believe the Story.

Abandoning Substitute Centers
Some Traditionals will be reticent to give up their interest in a *Substitute Center* (see Chapter 11). A focus on Christ and his Kingdom must relegate

end-times studies, creation/evolution debates, favorite theological positions, marriage/family issues, or politics to *secondary status.*

Additionally, worried Traditionals can have a new perspective about the state of the world, the nation, the decaying American culture, the economy, or who controls the White House, Supreme Court, and Congress. While all American Christians should vigorously engage in politics and cultural preservation as an expression of social justice, they do not need to do so from a posture of fear. It is *Jesus'* role to consummate his Kingdom. It will not be ushered in by Democrats or Republicans.

Nostalgic Eras
While the 1950s was a nostalgic era for many white evangelicals, it was far from ideal for the Black church in America. Other eras may hold nostalgia for Traditionals, but no era compares with the *future* hope that he has prepared for those who long for his appearing (2 Tim. 4.8, Rev. 21.1-5).

Shifting the Paradigm of the Pragmatic Method
Pragmatics will have the most difficultly re-shaping their identity based on *Sacred Roots* because pragmatism has become so ingrained in their psyche. Without knowing it, they utilize the *Marketing Concept* in almost every decision, so they need a whole new worldview. The Pragmatic has to throw years of assumptions overboard. For some, it may be as difficult as breaking an addiction.

For example, they may find it counter-intuitive to consider that attendance and budget are not sacred measuring tools. Rather than leaving the outcomes to God, Pragmatics tend to judge a ministry's legitimacy on measurable outcomes, especially attendance, buildings, and cash. If these are increasing, it is assumed ministry is effective, legitimate, and blessed.

Jethani said, "What if we are not the primary agents behind bountiful growth or its absence? What if we stopped judging ourselves and others based on outcomes which rightfully belong to God, and rediscovered the humility of the sower—the one who rises day and night, casts the seed upon the ground and marvels as it grows?"[137]

For Pragmatics who are on the brink of burnout, this paradigm shift may be a source of relief—and "just in the nick of time." In fact, it may seem "too good to be true" that the Pragmatic can actually get off the treadmill of "numbers as a measure of success."

Innovating Appropriately

Some Pragmatics may be tempted to use *Sacred Roots* as another way to appeal to the individual consumer. Their familiarity with the *Marketing Concept* will drive them to use narrative and mystery as tools to meet individual needs, or as a new way to package the message for mass appeal.

The challenge for Pragmatics is to *use* innovation without being *driven by it*. For example, David Wells said, "Relevance is not about … the hottest marketing trend, the latest demographic, the newest study on depression, what younger a generation thinks, Starbucks, or contemporary music … Studies on contemporary life, whether of a demographic or a psychological kind, ... are helpful in understanding the way life is in a (post)modern world, but these studies do not themselves give the church its agenda."[138] Innovation is not a bad thing when done properly, but only when Jesus has replaced "the customer" as King.

Give Me the Bottom Line

Another difficulty for Pragmatics will be conceptualizing how *Jesus was cropped from the picture,* since they are accustomed to short, simple, easy-to-communicate sound bites. Pragmatics want "the bottom line," so it may be overwhelming to keep their attention long enough to communicate the complexities of the *cropping and de-cropping processes.* Because SLIM assumptions run deep, people may have difficulty comprehending the profound differences between *my personal relationship* and *his Kingdom Story,* and gloss over the ideas too quickly.

In fact, the Pragmatics' impulse to jump to practical application will make it nearly impossible to clarify the differences between "personal relationship" and "the Kingdom Story." They will hastily ask, "Now what do I do?" Developing deep roots takes time and will not happen overnight. A better question is, "How can I live out this Kingdom identity?"

Accepting Suffering

Pragmatics may also find it difficult to embrace a theology of suffering. The Bible's sources of evil (the world, the flesh, and the devil) may be new to many Pragmatics, and disengaging them from a therapeutic mindset may prove daunting. In fact, some Pragmatics became Christians for the very purpose of evading hardship.

However, for those who have faced personal tragedies, a biblical understanding of suffering could be liberating. It should be a relief to know that difficulty, death, sickness, and unexplained pain are not necessarily the fault of the Pragmatic doing "something wrong."

<u>Anchoring the Emerging Method</u>

In some ways, the Emerging Church has the greatest potential to embody the Church's *Sacred Roots*. They already have a narrative view of the Scriptures and are willing to adopt pre-Reformation (and even ancient) practices. They are deeply committed to making Jesus central and living out his missional teachings in their lives together. Their openness to theological dialogue, and their appreciation of mystery, make them less defensive and entrenched than the Traditional and Pragmatic methods. Some Emergings are creating marvelous ways to express worship as "producers," in contrast to the consumer-orientation of the Pragmatics. In fact, a number of Emerging churches may have already begun formation of an identity based on the Church's *Sacred Roots.*[139]

Utilitarian

However, many Emergings will find it challenging to embrace these *Sacred Roots* since their commitment to ancient practices is more practical than theological.[140] There is an underlying *individualistic streak* in their worship experiments. At times, it appears that the *individual's expression* is more important than what is pleasing to God.

Further, the focus of Emerging church is *so* missional that they may overlook worship as a simple expression of appreciation for Jesus' accomplishments. Gibbs and Bolger exposed Emergings' utilitarianism when they said that spiritual activities are useful in providing spiritual stamina and sense of calling for mission.[141]

Jesus Cropped from the Picture

The Great Tradition provides the foundational support from which individual expression should be measured. Allegiance to Jesus starts with what God wants his "celebration" to be, not what the individual Emerging wants (see Chapter 6: Worship as Celebration).

Potential Cults

The Emergings' commitment to *following the life of Jesus* will not, by itself, provide enough foundational support to keep them rooted in orthodoxy. The Church of Jesus Christ of Latter-Day Saints (Mormons), Christian Scientists, and Jehovah's Witnesses exemplify how a simple affirmation of *Jesus* or *Jehovah* is insufficient to keep a group anchored to historic Christian faith.

Therefore, each Emerging church must "tie down" its theology to the Great Tradition or they will go the way of liberalism or become a cult that is an enemy of the very Jesus they are now trying to follow. Emergings are especially vulnerable to heresy because they center their theology around an *open conversation*.

Training the Next Generation

It is unclear how the Emerging Method will pass on its faith to their children. As a movement of young and middle-aged people, they may not have considered how to conduct Christian education for their children. Until children develop to the point where they can reason and reflect, they are unable to "enter a theological conversation," which is a key to the Emerging Method.

Children can experience life in the Christian community but they also *need to be told* what Christians believe. The Emergings' hesitancy to make such declarative statements, and their desire to make thin lines between those "inside and outside," make it challenging to provide comprehensible training for children. Embracing the Church's *Sacred Roots* can help in this regard.

Identification with Postmodernity

Some Emergings may feel the exhilaration of a fresh movement that is acceptable to popular culture. It may feel hip, cool, and chic. But the Emergings' emphasis on Postmodernity also puts them in a precarious position. When the freshness wears off, they may feel even more demoralized than before; lost and alone with no objective core.

The Traditionals have *the Bible and the Cross* under which they can "find shelter in a time of storm." Pragmatics have the *Marketing Concept* to help them navigate difficult waters when they are "lost at sea." Emergings have no such ideas to give them coherence, leaving them without a place of shelter or a "star to guide them by." Postmodernity, by its nature, does not give enough objective truth to form, or sustain, a movement. It leaves too much to the individual. The Great Tradition will always be a safe harbor to which worn-out Emergings can return.

Also, whenever missionaries start with a desire to be culturally relevant, they are in danger of becoming enslaved to that culture (syncretism). When people contextualize the Bible to culture without the wisdom handed down through the centuries, culture tends to overwhelm their theology. Churches must develop deep roots of identity that provide the resources necessary to connect with the culture *without being syncretistic.* Good mission strategy always *starts with the Great Tradition* and then contextualizes outward.

Belcher said, "It is as if the emerging churches want the fruit but not the roots from which it came. So in their attempt to be culturally relevant (which they are doing very well), their traditions are not strong enough, I fear, to resist being absorbed by the surrounding culture. There is simply not enough depth in the rituals, disciplines, and practices that are adopted."[142]

Emergings should be applauded for their passion to contextualize within Postmodernity. They exemplify the Holy Spirit's work to guide the Church in an emerging age. However, Emergings must learn from the mistakes of past missionaries who tried to import colonial European culture to Africa, or Jews who forced Gentiles to be circumcised before becoming Christians. Emerging missionaries who are sent to non-Western cultures could be shocked to discover that indigenous people, especially the poor, have no use for philosophical conversations about Modernity, but simply desire to ally themselves with the Story given in the Great Tradition. Churches must be planted with *indigenous* expression of culture, not Postmodern ones.

History has shown that the Church has faced multiple shifts in predominant philosophy (see Appendix 5, "Six Paradigms of History"). It is human nature to believe that the latest philosophy is the final one. But it is improbable that Postmodernity is the final era of human philosophy. Unless the Lord returns, some other philosophy is likely to overtake Postmodernity. Therefore, Emergings should hold Postmodernity loosely.

Other Cropping Dangers

Emergings are at risk to *crop Jesus from the picture* in two other ways. First, their Kingdom theology is primarily missional and rarely mentions the presence and engagement of evil. The powers of evil are often *cropped out* of their picture. Their distaste for nationalism and the Traditionals' alignment with conservative politics make the notion of "spiritual warfare" an unpleasant topic. But, like King Theoden in *Lord of the Rings,* this war has been thrust upon Emergings, whether they find it unpleasant or not.

Second, like the Traditionals' suspicion of pre-Reformation thought, Emergings are suspicious of the institutionalized church, which is also known as Christendom (see Appendix 5, "A Timeline of Other Historical Developments"). Their critique of recent Traditional or Pragmatic expressions is admirable, but Emergings must be careful not to *crop the Holy Spirit out of the picture,* who has been at work even in Christendom.

Finally, the Emergings' desire to embody Christ's teachings is an improvement from the privatized ethics of the other methods. However, if their "list" simply replaces the Pragmatic's "list," Jesus will end up being *cropped out of the picture* once again. It is not helpful to replace a *cross-only* theology with a *teaching-only* one. A multi-dimensional view of Christus Victor is the best way to prevent the *cropping effect.* There is no reason to pit Jesus' *teachings* against his substitutionary *work on the cross.* Both should be celebrated.

Freedom in Christ

Emergings who cannot moor themselves to the Great Tradition may stumble along the way. Like the Traditionals and Pragmatics, Emergings need to become *rooted, but not constrained.* They need to be free in Christ, but not *crop Jesus, or the devil's kingdom, from the picture.*

They are right to declare an *emerging* sense of the Holy Spirit's work in the Church throughout history, but that emergence flows from an *objective place,* like a tree whose *Sacred Roots* go deep into the ground and whose branches continue to grow in emerging ways.

Emergings who have the wisdom to anchor themselves to these *Sacred Roots* will be liberated to fully explore their existing commitments. Like Jazz musicians who ground themselves in a basic structure from which to innovate, Emergings attached to *Sacred Roots* can contextualize within Postmodernity, react against Christendom, follow Jesus and his teachings, worship as producers, and continue their theological conversation.

Conclusion

Jesus Cropped from the Picture is a story of the unintended consequences of well-meaning Christians desiring to fulfill the Great Commission. The church in America, once so dynamic, creative, and vigorous, is quickly becoming lethargic, lukewarm, and shallow as it blends Christian faith with contemporary marketing principles (syncretism). As a result, the common response is to employ a method to build the church, rather than return to the Church's *Sacred Roots.*

Identification with these *Sacred Roots* is <u>not</u> a method. It is not some clever campaign to re-invigorate the church for increased attendance, or to be relevant to contemporary culture. **It is a call to go back to something ancient, old, trusted, tried, and true.**

With its faithfulness to the Kingdom Story, an identity based on *Sacred Roots* can *liberate* the Traditional Method to greater fruitfulness, *shift the paradigm* for the Pragmatic Method so it can innovate appropriately, and *anchor* the Emerging Method so it can contextualize in missional community.

Forging an identity based on the Church's *Sacred Roots* allows churches to:

- Disengage from the cultural forces causing the American church to decline
- Re-connect to their historic, *Sacred Roots*
- Retain their distinctive heritage and expression
- Plant churches in indigenous cultures
- Become *People of the Story* in their theology, worship, discipleship, and outreach, to the glory of God.

The purpose of this book is not to fix the church, but to bring greater honor and glory to the Lord and Savior Jesus Christ. May he no longer be *cropped from the picture of his own Story.*

⛩

Our Father in heaven, hallowed be your name. Your Kingdom come, your will be done, on earth as in heaven. Give us today our daily bread. Forgive us our sins, as we forgive those who sin against us. Lead us not into temptation, but deliver us from evil. For the Kingdom, the power and the glory are yours. Now and for ever. Amen

Epilogue

Jesus Cropped from the Picture chronicles my journey from discouragement to joyful freedom; my experience with America's miniaturization of the Story, and the discovery that the Kingdom, expressed in the Great Tradition, is *the* antidote to the *cropping* process.

Constructing an identity based on the Church's *Sacred Roots* helps churches of all cultures to ground themselves in the Great Tradition, so the Church can be One, yet free to express its devotion within its indigenous culture. This has been God's intent since before the foundation of the world, revealed to Abraham, and fulfilled in Rev. 5.9.

Forming this identity is the way to restore bored Christians to vibrant faith. Identity produces life, but "how-to" methods crop Jesus from the picture. In fact, the subtitle, "How To Restore Them to Vibrant Faith" is a tongue-in-cheek reference to current tendencies to gravitate to the latest *how-to* method.

As founding Director of The Urban Ministry Institute (TUMI), Rev. Dr. Don Davis has invested decades of research and prayerful study to the Church's *Sacred Roots*, which is the foundation of TUMI's approach to urban church leadership development.

As TUMI's Satellite Director, I am honored to work under Dr. Davis' pioneering leadership to produce new resources that help churches anchor themselves to their *Sacred Roots*. Many resources already exist and can be found at our website, www.tumi.org, where we have dedicated a section to *Sacred Roots* ("Sacred Roots: Mobilize Urban Churches for Action").

Also, at www.tumi.org, the "TUMI Store" lists items to help in the dimensions of *theology, worship, discipleship,* and *outreach.* Here are some highlights:

⋄ Dr. Davis writes *The TUMI Annual* to provide weekly worship and preaching guidance for an entire year, where pastors can integrate a church's life of worship around the Great Tradition and an annual theme.

⋄ *Master the Bible* is a comprehensive Scripture memory system, using the Kingdom of God as its systematic orientation. There are 400 verses, each with their connection to the Kingdom Story. This material can also be used for follow-up and discipleship.

⋄ *The Capstone Curriculum* is TUMI's premier leadership development resource, a seminary-level certificate program for pastors, systematically rooted in the Kingdom of God and the Nicene Creed. This is available in English and Spanish and is delivered through one of our many local satellite campuses worldwide.

⋄ We also offer an *Urban Church Planting Manual* for those wanting to develop a strategic plan to plant churches. Dozens of church plant teams have benefitted from this material, across a number of denominational lines.

The Urban Ministry Institute is dedicated to facilitating church-plant movements around the world, especially for the poor. We are eager to help any church become better equipped in applying the Great Tradition. I pray that my testimony will whet your appetite to investigate the Church's *Sacred Roots* as **the way** to help your congregation become the *People of the Story*, where bored and discouraged Christians can find vibrant faith in Christ again. To God be the glory!

Appendices

Appendix 1: The Story God is Telling

The entire biblical account, from Genesis 3, where spiritual warfare began for humanity, to Revelation 20, where it ends even for Satan and his evil kingdom, expresses ongoing conflict between good and evil."

- Ed Murphy, The Handbook for Spiritual Warfare[143]

<u>God's Mysterious Strategy (Eph. 3.2-11)</u>

From the beginning there was a plan (Eph. 1.4)...

To invade the devil's kingdom, reversing the effects of the fall (Matt. 12.28-29)...

And rescue a people to be his own (1 Pet. 2.9-10)...

And empower his people to continue his work (John 14.12)...

Through the power of the Holy Spirit (Acts 1.8)...

Who would make steady progress defeating the enemy (Matt. 16.18)...

Until he comes to finish the job (Matt. 24.14, 30)...

And enjoy his family forever (Rev. 21.1-5).

The Story In Chapter Version

Chapter 1: An Attempted Coup (Before Time)
Biblical Period: Gen. 1.1a

God exists in perfect fellowship before creation. The devil and his followers rebel and bring evil into existence. *In the beginning was the Word, and the Word was with God, and the Word was God. He was in the beginning with God. All things were made through him, and without him was not any thing made that was made (John 1.1-3).*

See also Isa. 14.12-17, Ezek. 28.12-19, 2 Pet. 2.4

Chapter 2: Insurrection (Creation and The Fall)
Biblical Period: Gen. 1.1b-3.13

God creates man in his image who then joins Satan in rebellion. *Just as sin came into the world through one man, and death through sin, and so death spread to all men because all sinned (Rom. 5.12).*

See also 1 Cor. 15.21

Chapter 3: Preparing for Invasion (The Patriarchs, Kings, and Prophets)
Biblical Period: Gen. 3.14-Malachi

God contends to set apart a people for his own, out of which will come a King to deliver mankind, including Gentiles. Clues to his battle plans are hinted at along the way. *They are Israelites, and to them belong the adoption, the glory, the covenants, the giving of the law, the worship, and the promises. To them belong the patriarchs, and from their race, according to the flesh, is the Christ who is God over all (Rom. 9.4-5).*

See also Gen. 3.16, 12.1-3, 49.8-10, Exod. 14.13-14, 15.1-3, 19.3-6, 1 Sam. 17.45-47, 2 Sam. 7.12-16, Isa. 2.2-4, Joel 2.28-32, Amos 9.11-15, Mic. 1.2-4, Mal. 4.1-3

Chapter 4: Victory and Rescue (Incarnation, Temptation, Miracles, Resurrection)
Biblical Period: Matt. 1.1 - Acts 1.11

The Savior comes to deal a disarming blow to his enemy. *The reason the Son of God appeared was to destroy the works of the devil (1 John 3.8).*

See also Ps. 2.1-12, Isa. 61.1-4, Matt. 4.1-11, 11.12, 12.25-30, Mark. 1.14-15, 22, 27, Luke 1.31-35, 4.16-18, 11.14-28, 16.16, John 1.14-18, Rom. 5.1-2, 1 Cor. 2.6-8, Gal. 3.10-14, 4.4-5, Col. 1.13-14, 2.15, Heb. 2.14-15, 9.11-12

Chapter 5: The Army Advances (The Church)
Biblical Period: Acts 1.12-Rev. 3

The Savior reveals his plan of a people assigned to take progressive ownership from the enemy as they enjoy a foretaste of the Kingdom to come. *Through the Church the manifold wisdom of God might now be made known to the rulers and authorities in the heavenly places. This was according to the eternal purpose that he has realized in Christ Jesus our Lord (Ephesians 3.10-11).*

See also Matt. 10.34-39, 13.33, 16.18, 24.14, 28.18-20, Mark. 4.26-32, Luke 10.16-20, 17.20, Rom. 16.25-26, 2 Cor. 11.13-15, Eph. 1.9-12, 2.1-10, 3.4-6, Col. 1.26, 1 Tim. 1.18, 6.12, 2 Tim. 2.3-4, 1 Pet. 5.8-9

Chapter 6: The Final Conflict (The Second Coming)
Biblical Period: Rev. 4-22

The Savior returns to destroy his enemy, marry his Bride, and resume his rightful place on the throne. *Then comes the end, when he delivers the kingdom to God the Father after destroying every rule and every authority and power. For he must reign until he has put all his enemies under his feet. The last enemy to be destroyed is death (1 Cor. 15.24-26).*

See also Mark. 14.24-25, Rom. 16.20, 2 Pet. 3.7-13, Rev. 7.9, 11.15, 19.6-21, 20.7-10, 21.1-11, 22-26, 22.3-5

Appendix 2: The Church as Agent of the Kingdom

The Church is a community of people—past, present, and future, who have been called out of the kingdom of darkness through saving faith in Jesus Christ.

◇ One family, made up of all peoples, tribes, nations, and tongues (Gen. 12.1-3, Rev. 7.9)
◇ The people of God who will be blessed to be with him forever in glory (Rev. 21.3-4)
◇ The bride of Christ for whom he gave his life as a ransom (Rev. 21.2, Mark 10.45)
◇ The body of Christ over which Christ is head (Rom. 12.5, Eph. 1.22-23)
◇ Foreshadowed as far back as the Promise to Abraham (Gen. 12.3)
◇ An example of the blessings and wholeness of our fellowship in heaven. People can experience a glimpse of what heaven will be like by observing the Church's fellowship and good works (1 Pet. 2.9-10, Col. 3.12-16).

We are saved into a community.
Christianity is a team sport.

Appendix 3: His Seamless Plan

Creation: God existed in Triune community. Man was created in his image.

Fall: God's authority is challenged and the people join the revolt, and are enslaved to the enemy.

Plan: God' s rescue plan is announced (The seed of the woman will crush the serpent's head, Gen. 3.16).

People: Abraham and Israel are promised a multi-ethnic family (Gen. 12.1-3). A Jewish nation provides a heritage out of which the Church is later formed.

Person: The Jewish deliverer invades, robs the enemy's house (Matt. 12.29), and disarms the powers of evil (Col. 2.15, Heb. 2.14).

Nations: At Pentecost, a multi-national community is established to carry on his work (John 14.12). Christ's redemptive work has *no geographical bounds.*

Mystery Revealed: Christ establishes the Church as the continuation of his effort to destroy the devil's work. A temple is being built until the end when all cultures enter in (Matt. 24.14, Eph. 2.20-22). With the entry of Gentiles, Christ's redemptive work now has no *cultural bounds.* If the devil had known God's plan, he would not have crucified Christ (1 Cor. 2.7-8). This is the mystery of God's plan (Rom. 16.25, Eph. 1.9-10, 3.2-11, 5.32, 6.19, Col. 1.24-27, 2.2-3, Col. 4.3, 1 Tim. 3.16, Rev. 10.7).

Unfolding Story: The history of the Church fills in the missing part of the Bible's Story. In the Church Age, we continue Jesus' work of destroying the devil's work (1 John 3.8), winning back what was lost (Luke 19.10), under the headship of Christ.

Fulfillment: The King returns to finish what he started. All things are restored "under his feet." All the objectives of the Kingdom plan are complete, to the praise of his glory.

Everything is going according to plan, meeting all his Kingdom objectives,
even though it looks chaotic at times,
and much work and suffering must be endured until it is over.

Appendix 4: Contrasting Views of Worship Services

See Robert Webber's books:

Ancient Future Faith (Part Four) and *Ancient Future Worship* (Baker Books)

Purpose

SLIM   Worship helps **me** in my personal walk with Christ.

EPIC   Worship draws us into the celebration of **Jesus** who lived, died, overwhelmed the powers of darkness; who works in our lives today in the midst of spiritual warfare; who is coming again to rescue us and put an end to evil, restoring his rightful place on the throne (Christus Victor).

Prayer

SLIM   Prayer needs to hold **my** attention.

EPIC   Prayer takes our minds off ourselves as we seek **God** in the midst of a spiritual battle we fight together.

Singing

SLIM   Singing should be meaningful to **me** so I can worship God from my heart, and prepare to listen to the sermon.

EPIC   Singing focuses on the celebration of Christus Victor that draws our attention to **Christ**.

Sermon

SLIM   Sermons should be presented well so I can know more about the Bible, live a better life, and leave with a practical idea to cope with the difficulty of **my** week.

EPIC   Sermons remind us of the largeness of the Story of **Christ**, the many aspects of Christus Victor, so we find our identity in his Story. We need to be reminded of the many stories of his salvation given in his Word.

Jesus Cropped from the Picture

Central element

SLIM The sermon is the central element of the service.

EPIC Celebration of Christ's accomplishments is the central element of the service, of which the sermon is only one part.

Communion

SLIM Communion helps me remember how much Christ loves **me**.

EPIC Communion is a mysterious dramatization that reminds us of Jesus work to defeat the enemy and rescue a people to be his own; his real and powerful presence in the Church today; his imminent return to take the throne and receive the Church at the wedding banquet.

Baptism

SLIM Baptism is something **I** do to express **my** personal relationship with Christ.

EPIC Baptism is a command of Christ to show a change of allegiance from the kingdom of darkness to the Kingdom of God; from partnership with the world to divine connection to the body of Christ; from living for self to a life of union to the suffering, death, and resurrection of Christ.

Pastor

SLIM A pastor facilitates **my** personal relationship with Christ by providing for **my** feeding.

EPIC A pastor mobilizes the church as the army representing Christ in a community, reminding the people of their identity as *People of the Story*.

Goal

SLIM Everything is done with excellence so I can invite others to come and have their **needs** met. "We need to fill those seats!"

EPIC Everything is done to point to the Story of a God who acted, is active, and is coming again to fulfill all things, so we can be faithful to the Story. "We need to be focused on Christ, even if no one else comes."

Evaluation

SLIM   1) How much did I get from the sermon?
            2) How uplifted do I feel after the service?
            3) How much did I learn?

EPIC   1) Did we experience God together?
            2) How much bigger did God become in relation to me?
            3) How prepared am I to be faithful to the Story?

Prominent Terminology

SLIM   **I/me/personal** (Christ is cropped from the picture)

EPIC   Christ/Church/powers of evil

Appendix 5: Bringing History Together

This selective review of history is intended to describe the development of the Traditional, Pragmatic, and Emerging methods. It is impossible to provide a single summary of 2000 years of Church history with any integrity, so instead, four contrasting historical developments are summarized:

⋄ Six Paradigms of Church History (Robert Webber)
⋄ Views of the Atonement (Gustav Aulen)
⋄ The Splintering of Western Protestantism (Robert Webber and David Wells)
⋄ A Timeline of Key Historical Events

<u>Six Paradigms of History</u>[144]

Biblical period (0-100). The predominant philosophy was an *holistic* understanding of the world, where God was at work, as recorded in the Old Testament. The emphasis was on the history, rites, and rituals handed down from God to the Jews, a <u>community</u> out of which the Church was birthed at Pentecost and apostolic faith established.

The Ancient Period (100-600) was formed by Platonic thought, namely that universals are of another world and this world is a shadow of that other reality. The Church emphasized the <u>mystery</u> of how the Church represents the reality of heaven. The Eastern Orthodox tradition has stayed consistent with the practices of the Ancient Period, and finds its identity in connecting with the aspect of "mystery" that was emphasized in that age.

The Medieval period (600-1500) embraced Aristotle's philosophy that universals are seen in creation, and that the Church was visible as an institution. The Roman Catholic Church embodied this belief, with its emphasis on <u>institution</u> and organization, which continues today.

The Reformation (1500-1750) was based on nominalism, the belief that Truth is found in the mind. The mind was recognized as the highest faculty of man, who is created in God's image. People began to believe less in Aristotle's inherent universals, and more that something was true because "God said it was true." As individuals were able to read, and the authority of the Roman Catholic institution diminished, the <u>Bible</u> took center stage as the primary source of authority. The Church turned to the Bible as an object of study, allowing individuals to interpret what they were reading. It can be inferred that individualism began during this period.

The view of God shifted from a "God who acts in history as Christus Victor" (the predominant view of the Church for the first 1000 years), to a "God who speaks through his written Word." The Bible began to be understood as "the mind of God" in written form. Truth was known as the human mind met God's mind, through the Scriptures. The Bible began to be understood as a set of observable data leading to rational answers, which could be described using propositional statements.

In reaction to abuses within Catholicism, the Reformation contributed to a high view of Scripture and personal salvation by grace, through faith. With a new understanding of the Church,

Protestants turned away from the Church as the *presence of God in history*, and concentrated on its calling to proclaim the gospel. The Reformed traditions were founded during this time and continue today.

The Modern period (1750-1980) was based on <u>reason</u>, illustrated by Descartes who famously said, "I think, therefore I am." This period also coincides with the era known as the Enlightenment, which emphasized empirical data through scientific methods, leading to rational answers to mysterious questions. This carried into the Western church, so that by the 1800s Protestants split into two groups over the proper application of reason: liberals (who denied the supernatural on scientific grounds) and conservatives (who used reason to develop a proof-oriented faith). The development of the scientific method resulted in dramatic improvements in the human condition, widespread missionary activity, and accessible biblical scholarship. Liberal (or Social Action) traditions, as well as Conservative (Fundamental and Evangelical) traditions were formed during this time. This is the time frame where the Traditional and Pragmatic methods were born.

The Postmodern period (1980-present) formed out of the breakdown of confidence in reason and science. There is greater value placed on subjective <u>experience</u> than objective data and analytical methods. Postmoderns believe that the link between propositional statements and the meaning behind them has been severed, so objective truth should be viewed with suspicion. Therefore, the language of "truth" needs to be explored by each individual. The Emerging Method comes out of this paradigm of history.

In all six periods, Christian faith has been partially *formed* by the cultural philosophy surrounding it, while the church has also *affected* the surrounding culture. There has never been a time where the Bible has been lived out in a cultural vacuum. But sometimes culture encroached so far (syncretism) that corrective action was required.

Views of the Atonement[145]

There are three historical views of Jesus' atonement that have shaped later views.

The Classic View (Christus Victor) was held by the Church for the first 1000 years of its history, which included the apostles and Church fathers. Its focus was on Christ, the Victorious Champion, where men and women were the prize to be won from the clutches of the powers of evil. It was written in dramatic, narrative style, emphasizing all the works of Christ to defeat the enemy including his birth, death, temptation, miracles, resurrection, ascension, and Second Coming. For the believer, salvation was only the beginning of a life doing battle against the enemy. Baptism was an act of entering into the community of Jesus, joining with the rest of the Church to engage in conflict against the kingdom of darkness.

The Latin (Objective) View came into wide acceptance during the medieval period, with the writings of Anselm (1033-1109). He provided "a logical explanation for the necessity of Jesus Christ's death on the cross. He used a framework and imagery taken, not from the Bible, but from the feudalistic system of his day ... He sought to interpret the cross with images easily intelligible to the people of his era."[146]

Anselm emphasized Christ's substitution at the cross as a debt owed to God by sinful humanity. This legal approach was consistent with contemporary ideas about jurisprudence.

The Subjective (Humanistic) View of Abelard (1079-1142), coincided with Anselm (Latin View). While Anselm's Latin View recognized a payment of debt (an objective transaction outside of humanity), Abelard's Subjective View emphasized the change *inside* a person because of Jesus' sacrificial work at the cross. "For Abelard, the cross was not so much about removing an objective barrier between God and humans but rather a demonstration to humanity of God's matchless love."[147] Christ was seen as the loving servant-teacher. Instead of a legal transaction where man exchanged repentance for justification, Abelard emphasized that man should offer repentance in order to be empowered lead a good life. This view took root in liberalism in the 1900s and continues in the Social Justice tradition today.

Later One-Dimensional Views

Anselm and Abelard presented two different "one-dimensional" views of the work of Jesus. Each one presented a single reason for Christ's work, rather than highlighting it as *one of the many victories* of Christ. Theologians who came later continued this "one-dimensional" approach and postulated other views of the atonement, such as the penal substitution view (Charles Hodge, 1797-1878).[148] Variations of Hodge's view have persisted to the present day.

Since Anselm and Abelard, the Classic View (Christus Victor) fell by the wayside, although Luther attempted to give it new life[149] (see the lyrics of *A Mighty Fortress is Our God*). But the Christus Victor view became a footnote to the Reformation and never regained prominence. In the West, Jesus' death on the cross has represented the atonement ever since.

The Splintering of Western Protestantism

David Wells[150] and Robert Webber[151] provide excellent historical analysis regarding the development of the Traditional, Pragmatic, and Emerging methods (see Figure 22).

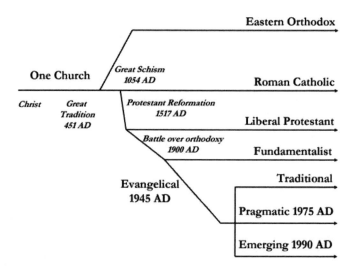

Figure 22: The Three Methods

In the mid-1800s, "The Battle Over Orthodoxy" ensued over the application of Rationalism. Liberals attempted to make Christianity palatable to the cultural elite and the highly educated. Overwhelmed by the fear of being irrelevant to the Enlightenment culture who were respected in the universities, literature, arts, and sciences, liberals sought an intellectual truce. From this compromise, a synthesis of

Christianity and secular humanism was born.[152] Liberals used Rationalism to question the trustworthiness of the Bible, and emphasized the love of God and Jesus' moral teaching over his substitutionary work at the cross (Abelard). They viewed Christianity as more about life than doctrine; more about deeds than creeds.

Conservatives reacted against liberalism, retaining a high view of Scripture, and emphasizing the wrath of God that was satisfied in Jesus' death on the cross (Anselm and Hodge). They viewed liberalism as a dangerous blending of cultural Rationalism with Christian practice (syncretism).

By the early 20th century, after separating themselves from liberalism, conservatives started a new dialogue among themselves regarding the degree to which they should specify the limits of definitive, authentic, biblical faith. Some thought historic orthodoxy should affirm a long list of fundamentals, and were more willing to retreat within themselves rather than be polluted by the world. Others thought there should be more outreach to the world and openness to differences within Christian traditions. Those who pressed for more flexibility became known as evangelicals, and those who stayed committed to a longer list of fundamental principles were called fundamentalists. By World War II, evangelicals had significantly separated from fundamentalists.

In the decades after World War II, evangelicals split into three competing groups, each reacting against the previous one. In general, Traditional evangelicals are those who came to faith from 1950-1975. They maintain that Christian faith "makes sense," focusing on Josh McDowell-style apologetics (*Evidence That Demands a Verdict*). Their paradigm of church is institutional, neighborhood-oriented, and civic in nature. Sometimes being a good citizen is equated to being a good Christian. The leader is the pastor-preacher, the "man in the pulpit." For them, youth ministry is church-centered, with education coming primarily from Sunday school or youth group. Spirituality is defined by "keeping the rules," and music preferences include hymns or choruses from the 1700s-1960s.

Traditional evangelicals became the foil against which Pragmatic evangelicals reacted. Pragmatics came to faith from 1975-2000, with a commitment to a Christianity "that works," (instead of the Traditional's view that it "made sense"). Pragmatics emphasized that God had meaning for an individual's life, with a "plan for your life." The church was market-driven and consumer-oriented, moving from "neighborhood" church to "mega church," where a variety of programs could be offered to attract people. Pastoral leadership moved from the "pastor-preacher" to the "effective manager." Youth ministry shifted from "Christian education" to "fun activities designed to keep young people out of trouble." Target groups were segmented so their felt needs could be met. Spirituality moved from "keeping the rules" to "experiencing blessing and success." The worship style become more contemporary, keeping with the popular music style of the 1970s and 1980s.

In general, Emerging (Younger) evangelicals are those who came to faith after 2000, reacting to both Traditional and Pragmatic evangelicals. Their theological commitments were formed out of a hunger for relevance in Postmodern culture. They care less about reason or pragmatism, but are on a quest for personal meaning through a missional lifestyle. They opt for small, inter-cultural communities of faith over large, homogenous ones. They also prefer less hierarchical leadership structures and value participation. Youth ministry is more outreach focused, with education offered through informal and inter-generational contact. Their worship is more reflective and personalized, seeking authentic spirituality.

<u>A Timeline of Other Historical Developments</u>

313   **The Ascent of Emperor Constantine:** Constantine was the Emperor of Rome from 306 A.D., and the undisputed holder of that office from 324 until his death in 337. In 313, he ended many years of official persecution toward the Church, proclaimed religious toleration throughout the empire, and professed personal faith in Christ. No longer under siege, the Church was abruptly propelled into prominence. Some Christians assert that the Church was healthy and vibrant before Constantine, but became stagnant after Constantine legitimized and institutionalized it. Some Christian leaders point to Constantine as a turning point in Church history from which the Church has yet to recover.[153]

0-451   **The Great Tradition:** The Great Tradition represents the central core of Christian belief and practice, derived from the Scriptures, that runs from the time of Christ to the middle of the fifth century. Most of what has been proven essential and foundational to theology, spirituality, and witness was articulated by the Church in its life together, its cannon (Scripture), creeds, and councils. All the later expressions of Christian faith have their roots in the Great Tradition (Eastern Orthodox, Roman Catholic, Reformed, Evangelical, Emerging, Social Justice, Charismatic, Fundamentalist, Sacramental).

1000-1100 **Anselm and Abelard** suggested differing views regarding a *single* purpose of Jesus' atonement, beginning the process of neglecting the Christus Victor view as the Church's primary hermeneutic.

1500-1750 **The Reformation** focused on the Bible and salvation by grace through faith as corrections to Roman Catholicism.

1730-1840 The Great Awakenings in America (**Frontier Revivalism**) focused on personal salvation and inner-reflection.

1850-1945 Protestants split between **liberal and conservative** traditions.

1945-1975 **Evangelicalism** formed and the *Marketing Concept* took hold in American culture.

1975-1990 The **Pragmatic Method** formed in an effort to more effectively market Christian faith. Those who resisted pragmatic assumptions could be included in the Traditional Method.

1990-Present The **Emerging Method** formed to contextualize Christian faith in a Postmodern environment, rejecting many of the Traditional and Pragmatic assumptions and methodologies.

Suggested Reading

Those interested in further study may find the following books helpful. I have listed them from *simplest* to *most challenging.*

Eldredge, John. *Epic.* Nashville, TN: Thomas Nelson, 2004.

Webber, Robert. *Who Gets to Narrate the World?* Downers Grove, IL: InterVarsity Press, 2008.

White, John. *The Fight.* Downers Grove, IL: InterVarsity Press, 1976.

Jethani, Skye. *The Divine Commodity,* Grand Rapids, MI: Zondervan, 2009.

Curtis, Brent and John Eldredge. *The Sacred Romance.* Nashville, TN: Thomas Nelson Publishers, Inc., 1997.

Hauerwas, Stanley, and William H. Willimon. *Resident Aliens.* Nashville, TN: Abingdon Press, 1998.

Ladd, George. *The Gospel of the Kingdom.* Grand Rapids, MI: Wm. B. Eerdmans Publishing Co., Reprinted 1999.

DeYoung, James, and Sarah Hurty. *Beyond the Obvious.* Gresham, OR: Vision House Publishing, 1995.

Wright, Christopher. *Knowing Jesus Through the Old Testament.* Downers Grove, IL: InterVarsity Press, 1992.

Belcher, Jim. *Deep Church.* Downers Grove, IL: InterVarsity Press, 2009.

Dudley, Guilford. *The Recovery of Christian Myth.* Eugene, OR: Wipf & Stock Publishing. The Westminster Press, 1967.

Webber, Robert. *Ancient Future Faith.* Grand Rapids, MI: Baker Books, 2008.

Murphy, Ed. *The Handbook of Spiritual Warfare.* Nashville, TN: Thomas Nelson Publishers, Inc., 2003.

Aalen, Gustaf. *Christus Victor.* Eugene, OR: Wipf & Stock Publishers, 1931.

Ladd, George. *The Presence of the Future.* New York: Harper and Row, 1974.

Endnotes

[1] Wood, Rick. March-April 2008. *Are We Proclaiming a Defective Gospel.* Mission Frontiers, page 9.

[2] *A Presbytery Handbook for Creating New Churches*, Chapter 6, page 36.

[3] Barna, George. *Revolution.* Carol Stream, IL: Tyndale House Publishers, Inc., 2005, page 2.

[4] McNeal, Reggie. *New Reality Number One: The Collapse of the Church Culture.* http://media.wiley.com/product_data/excerpt/85/07879656/0787965685.pdf, page 4.

[5] Wells, David. *The Courage to be Protestant.* Grand Rapids, MI: Wm. B. Eerdmans Publishing Co., 2008, page 48.

[6] Roberts, Bob. *The Multiplying Church.* Grand Rapids, MI: Zondervan, 2008, page 25.

[7] This production was adapted from the 1991 Disney movie, *Beauty and the Beast*, DVD, directed by Gary Trousdale (1991; Burbank, CA: Walt Disney Video, 2002).

[8] Lewis, C.S. *Mere Christianity.* New York: HaperCollins, 1952, page 46.

[9] Horton, Michael. *Christless Christianity.* Grand Rapids, MI: Baker Books, 2008, page 30.

[10] *How to Know God Personally*, http://www.ccci.org/wij/index.aspx.

[11] Horton, Michael. *Christless Christianity*, page 18.

[12] Barna, George. *Revolution*, page 29, 37, 66, 115-16.

[13] Fee, Gordon. *A Happy Church.* http://www.gatewayboston.org/resources/happy_church.doc, page 6.

[14] This is my own summary from Clapp, Rodney. *A Peculiar People.* Downers Grove, IL: InterVarsity Press, 1996, Chapter 6: The Church as Worshiping Community, pages 94-113.

[15] Roberts, Bob. *The Multiplying Church*, page 18.

[16] *Drive Through Church*, http://www.youtube.com/watch?v=n4QFKS4LzS4.

[17] DeYoung, James, and Sarah Hurty. *Beyond the Obvious*. Gresham, OR: Vision House Publishing, 1995, pages 83-84.

[18] Ed Murphy provides an interesting and comprehensive, book-by-book commentary on the role of the devil throughout the Bible. Murphy, Ed. *The Handbook of Spiritual Warfare*. Nashville, TN: Thomas Nelson Publishers, Inc., 2003.

[19] An excellent place to start is Ladd, George. *The Gospel of the Kingdom*. Grand Rapids, MI: Wm. B. Eerdmans Publishing Co., Reprinted 1999.

[20] Snyder, Howard. *The Community of the King*. Downers Grove, IL: InterVarsity Press, 2004, page 65.

[21] Murphy, Ed. *The Handbook of Spiritual Warfare*. See also Matt. 4.1-11, 10.1, Luke 10.1-20, 11.20-22, Rom. 8.34, 1 Cor. 15.17-21, Col. 2.14-15, Heb. 2.17-18, 7.25, 1 John 2.1-2, Rev. 19.11-21.

[22] Webber, Robert. *Ancient Future Worship*. Grand Rapids, MI: Baker Books, 2008, page 143.

[23] Aalen, Gustaf. *Christus Victor*. Eugene, OR: Wipf & Stock Publishers, 1931.

[24] Webber, Robert. *Ancient Future Faith*. Grand Rapids, MI: Baker Books, 2008, pages 25, 44.

[25] Webber, Robert. *Ancient Future Faith*, page 41.

[26] Curtis, Brent and John Eldredge. *The Sacred Romance*. Nashville, TN: Thomas Nelson Publishers, Inc., 1997, page 81.

[27] DeYoung and Hurty. *Beyond the Obvious*, page 88.

[28] Dudley, Guilford. *The Recovery of Christian Myth*. Eugene, OR: Wipf & Stock Publishing. The Westminster Press, 1967, pages 1-58.

[29] Murphy, Ed. *The Handbook of Spiritual Warfare*, page 90.

[30] Wood, Rick. *Are We Proclaiming a Defective Gospel?*, page 10.

[31] Schaeffer, Francis. *The Complete Works of Francis Schaeffer, Volume 2: Joshua and the Flow of Biblical History*, Westchester, IL: Crossway Books, 1975, page 210.

[32] White, John. *The Fight*. Downers Grove, IL: InterVarsity Press, 1976, page 78.

[33] Dr. Don Davis frequently makes mention of this truth from a quote from Papias (see http://www.newadvent.org/fathers/01225.htm).

[34] Webber, Robert. *Ancient Future Faith*, page 197.

[35] Ibid.

[36] Ibid.

[37] Horton, Michael. *Christless Christianity*, page 146.

[38] Webber, Robert. *Ancient Future Worship*, page 174.

[39] Horton, Michael. *Christless Christianity*, page 142.

[40] Viola, Frank. *Pagan Christianity*. Tyndale House Publishers, Inc., 2008, page 230.

[41] Webber, Robert. *Ancient Future Faith*, page 134.

[42] Horton, Michael. *Christless Christianity*, page 20.

[43] Batterson, Mark. *Wild Goose Chase*. Colorado Springs, CO: Multnomah Books, 2008, page 72.

[44] To grow in understanding of Christ as the **SUBJECT** of the Old Testament, read Wright, Christopher. *Knowing Jesus Through the Old Testament*. Downers Grove, IL: InterVarsity Press, 1992.

[45] Webber, Robert. *Ancient Future Worship*, pages 33, 129.

[46] Curtis, Brent and John Eldredge. *The Sacred Romance*, page 45.

[47] EPIC is adapted from Leonard Sweet's writing (www.leonardsweet.com), represented by *Experiential, Participative, Image-rich, and Connective*. In my use of the acrostic, I used "Christ-centered" instead of "Connective."

[48] Wells, David. *The Courage to be Protestant*, page 140.

[49] Curtis, Brent and John Eldredge. *The Sacred Romance*, page 43.

[50] Davis, Don. *Our Declaration of Dependence: Freedom in Christ*, http://www.tumi.org/migration/images/stories/pdf/ourdeclofdependence.pdf.

[51] Webber, Robert. *Ancient Future Worship*, pages 115-116, 128.

[52] Batterson, Mark. *Wild Goose Chase*, page 171.

[53] Stevens, R. Paul. *The Equipper's Guide to Every Member Ministry*. Downers Grove, IL: InterVarsity Press, 1992, page 90.

[54] Roberts, Bob. *The Multiplying Church*, page 111.

[55] Stevens, R. Paul. *The Equipper's Guide to Every Member Ministry*, page 95.

[56] Frost, Michael and Alan Hirsch. *The Shaping of Things to Come*. Peabody, MA: Hendrickson Publishers, LLC, 2003, page 217.

[57] Viola, Frank. *Pagan Christianity*, page 99.

[58] Jethani, Skye. *The Divine Commodity*. Grand Rapids, MI: Zondervan, 2008, page 97.

[59] Hauerwas, Stanley, and William H. Willimon. *Resident Aliens*. Nashville, TN: Abingdon Press, 1998, pages 112-127.

[60] Frost, Michael and Alan Hirsch. *The Shaping of Things to Come*, page 208.

[61] Wells, David. *The Courage to be Protestant*, page 63.

[62] Webber, Robert. *Ancient Future Faith*, page 152.

[63] Batterson, Mark. *Wild Goose Chase*, page 160.

[64] White, John. *The Fight*, pages 216-217.

[65] Webber, Robert. *Ancient Future Faith*, pages 155-157.

[66] Horton, Michael. *Christless Christianity*, page 148, 150.

[67] Curtis and Eldredge. *The Sacred Romance*, pages 137, 144.

[68] Hauerwas and Willlimon. *Resident Aliens*, page 59.

[69] Eldredge, John. *Epic*. Nashville, TN: Thomas Nelson, 2004.

[70] Phillips, Keith. *Out of Ashes*. Los Angeles, CA: World Impact Press, 1996, page 47.

[71] The Pietistic and Puritan movements also had significant influence in these developments.

[72] *The Marketing Concept,* http://www.netmba.com/marketing/concept/.

[73] Kotler, Philip. *Marketing Management.* Fifth Edition, Englewood Cliffs, NJ: Prentice Hall, Inc., 1984, page 22.

[74] Wells, David. *The Courage to be Protestant*, page 53.

[75] Viola, Frank. *Pagan Christianity*, pages 65-72.

[76] Ibid., page 69.

[77] Ibid., page 69-71.

[78] Horton, Michael. *Christless Christianity*, page 58.

[79] David Wells has an extensive analysis of the Pragmatic Method, which he calls "Marketers" in his book, *The Courage to Be Protestant.*

[80] Horton, Michael. *Christless Christianity*, page 49.

[81] Jethani, Skye. *The Divine Commodity*, page 98.

[82] Ibid., page 109.

[83] Wells, David. *The Courage to be Protestant*, page 40.

[84] Ibid., page 25.

[85] Halter, Hugh. *The Tangible Kingdom*, San Francisco, CA: Jossey-Bass, 2008, pages 56-57.

[86] *A Shocking "Confession" from Willow Creek Community Church*, http://www.crosswalk.com/pastors/11558438/.

[87] Ibid.

[88] Postmoderns believe that the link between propositional statements and the meaning behind them has been severed, so objective truth should be viewed with suspicion. Therefore, the language of "truth" needs is to be explored by each individual.

[89] Gibbs, Eddie and Ryan Bolger. *Emerging Churches.* Grand Rapids, MI: Baker Academic, 2005, page 39.

[90] Ibid., page 78.

[91] McKnight, Scot. February 2007. *Five Streams of the Emerging Church*. Christianity, http://www.christianitytoday.com/ct/2007/february/11.35.html.

[92] Wells, David. *The Courage to be Protestant*, page 87.

[93] Ibid., page 46.

[94] Ibid., page 68.

[95] Gibbs, Eddie and Ryan Bolger. *Emerging Churches*, page 48.

[96] Ibid., page 93.

[97] Ibid., page 161.

[98] Ibid., page 23.

[99] Ibid., page 106.

[100] For example, *Peculiar People* (Rodney Clapp), *The Shaping of Things to Come* (Michael Frost and Alan Hirsch), *Pagan Christianity* (Frank Viola), or *The Tangible Kingdom* (Hugh Halter).

[101] Gibbs, Eddie and Ryan Bolger. *Emerging Churches*, pages 43-53.

[102] Ibid., pages 34-39.

[103] Ibid., page 21.

[104] Ibid., page 44.

[105] Horton, Michael. *Christless Christianity*, page 115.

[106] Gibbs, Eddie and Ryan Bolger. *Emerging Churches*, page 45.

[107] Ibid., pages 44, 50-51.

[108] Webber, Robert. *Ancient Future Worship*, page 170.

[109] Webber, Robert. *Ancient Future Faith*, page 17.

[110] Wells, David. *The Courage to be Protestant*, page 243.

[111] *Back to the Future*, DVD, directed by Robert Zemeckis (1985; Universal City, CA: Universal Studios, 2009).

[112] Davis, Don. *Sacred Roots: Mobilize Urban Churches for Action,* http://www. tumi.org/migration/index.php?option=com_content&view =Article&id=706&Itemid=691.

[113] Davis, Don. http://www.tumi.org/migration/Index.php?option =com_content&view=article&id=706&Itemid=691.

[114] Allsman, Don. *My Thoughts on the Creed,* http://www.tumi.org/forum /showpost.php?p=319&postcount=7.

[115] Webber, Robert. *Ancient Future Faith*, page 182.

[116] Lewis, C.S. *Mere Christianity*, page xv.

[117] Kotler, Philip. *Marketing Management,* pages 251-252.

[118] It can be argued that there are rare exceptions, such as the Monophysites and Monothelites.

[119] Eldredge. John. *Epic*, pages 11-13.

[120] Cavanaugh, Brian. *Picturing the Kingdom of God*, http://www.appleseeds.org/ picture.htm.

[121] *Theologians*, http://scandalon.co.uk/theology/bultmann.htm.

[122] Or "kakos." See Mark.4.15, John. 8.44, 2 Cor. 2.11, 11.14, 12.7, Eph. 4.27, 1 Tim. 4.1, 2 Tim. 2.26, 1 Pet. 5.8, 1 John 4.1-4.

[123] Or "kosmos." See Matt. 4.8-10, John 12.31, 14.30, 16.11, 2 Cor. 4.3-4, James 4.4-5, 1 John 2.15-17, 4.1-4, 5.19.

[124] Or "sarx." See Rom. 3.23, 5.19, 8.1-4, Eph. 2.3, 1 Tim. 3.6-9, 5.9, 14-15, 2 Tim. 2.14, 26, 1 Pet. 2.11, 5.5-11. All three are mentioned in James 4.1-11.

[125] Murphy, Ed. *The Handbook of Spiritual Warfare*, page 521.

[126] Murphy, Ed. *The Handbook of Spiritual Warfare*, page 61.

[127] *W. Russell Maltby Famous Quotes*, http://www.quotemountain.com/ Famous_quote_author/w_russell_maltby_famous_quotations/.

[128] DeYoung and Hurty. *Beyond the Obvious*, page 96.

[129] White, John. *The Fight*, page 222.

[130] Ibid., pages 224-225.

[131] DeYoung and Hurty. *Beyond the Obvious*, page 212.

[132] Foster, Richard. *Streams of Living Water*. New York: HaperCollins Publishers, 1998.

[133] While worship is expressed in narrow terms here, worship should be understood to encompass all aspects of individual and community life, whether it is theology, discipleship, outreach, or worship (in the narrow sense). Everything should be done for the glory of God and to defeat the adversary's kingdom.

[134] Brown, Brad. "Out on a Limb!" (sermon, Emmanuel Church, Burbank, CA, August 9, 2009).

[135] Davis, Don. http://www.tumi.org/migration/index.php?option= com_content&view=article&id=706&Itemid=691.

[136] Webber, Robert. *Ancient Future Faith*, pages 179, 185.

[137] Jethani, Skye. *The Divine Commodity*, page 186.

[138] Wells, David. *The Courage to be Protestant*, page 227.

[139] Jim Belcher's book, *Deep Church: A Third Way Beyond Emerging and Traditional* (Downers Grove, IL: InterVarsity Press, 2009) is a wonderful expression of a desire for a return to the Great Tradition. However, his subtitle suggests the Great Tradition as another method to resolve differences between Emergings and Traditionals in dominant-culture America. A commitment to the Church's *Sacred Roots* should not be seen as a method to resolve a particular sub-cultural situation, but rather is an attempt to retrieve the Great Tradition for the purposes of forming every congregation (in all cultures worldwide) into the *People of the Story*.

[140] Gibbs, Eddie and Ryan Bolger. *Emerging Churches*, page 219.

[141] Ibid., p. 223.

[142] Belcher, Jim. *Deep Church*, pages 133, 153.

[143] Murphy, Ed. *The Handbook of Spiritual Warfare*, page 521.

[144] Webber, Robert. *Ancient Future Faith,* pages 13-34.

[145] See Gustaf Aulen's *Christus Victor* and Robert Webber's *Ancient Future Faith.*

[146] Green, Joel. *Recovering the Scandal of the Cross.* Downers Grove, IL: InterVarsity Press, 2000, page 131.

[147] Ibid., p. 138.

[148] Ibid., p. 142-150.

[149] Aalen, Gustav. *Christus Victor*, pages 101-122.

[150] Wells (*The Courage to be Protestant*) calls these movements "Truth-Lovers, Marketers, and Emergents."

[151] Webber calls them "Traditional, Pragmatic, and Younger evangelicals." *An Interview with Robert Webber, author of The Younger Evangelicals*, http://www.theooze.com/articles/article.cfm?id=385&page=2.

[152] Wells, David. *The Courage to Be Protestant*, page 49.

[153] For example, Viola, Frank. *Pagan Christianity.*